the
omg
effect

'You're a breath of fresh air.'

'This is so universally applicable. Your sermons reach far and wide and are so healing. **I needed to hear this today**.'

'I've always been more spiritual than religious and veered away from the church, but **you bring such love and light** energy to the world.'

'I'm an atheist and I'd have a pint with Rev Chris. **He has a good heart**.'

'**Rev Chris is the wholesome kind of positivity this world needs.** I'm not even a religious person, and I'm over here nodding along like I know the good word.'

'**You are the only Christian I can stand**, tbh.'

'I'm not Christian but I always receive **positive vibes** from your account.'

'I'm not spiritual or anything. But I love your sermons because it still **applies to life** anyways.'

'Keep spreading those positive vibes, **we need more people like you Rev Chris!!**'

Rev. Chris Lee

the omg
effect

C

CENTURY

1 3 5 7 9 10 8 6 4 2

Century
20 Vauxhall Bridge Road
London SW1V 2SA

Century is part of the Penguin Random House group of companies whose
addresses can be found at global.penguinrandomhouse.com.

Penguin
Random House
UK

First published by Century in 2020

www.penguin.co.uk

A CIP catalogue record for this book is available from the British Library.
The author and publishers disclaim, as far as the law allows, any liability arising directly or
indirectly from the use or misuse of the information contained in this book.

ISBN 9781529125757

Printed and bound in Great Britain by Clays Ltd, Elcograf S.p.A.

The authorised representative in the EEA is Penguin Random House Ireland,
Morrison Chambers, 32 Nassau Street, Dublin D02 YH68.

Penguin Random House is committed to a sustainable future for
our business, our readers and our planet. This book is made
from Forest Stewardship Council® certified paper.

the omg
effect

To my extraordinary wife Jenny,
my life and silly-dance partner

A NOTE ON THE 60-SECOND
SERMONS

A couple of years ago, I began recording a series of short videos, sixty seconds or so long, and posted them to Instagram. I wanted to offer people a meaningful message of love and hope, and try to encourage anyone watching that they are of great value, and they're loved, and that there is always hope for them. I was overwhelmed by the positive responses I received, as people from all walks of life and religious beliefs found moments of connection and hope in these small sermons. I realised that I had this amazing opportunity: I was able to reach out and speak to thousands of people who wouldn't dream of setting foot inside a church building. I could speak life and light into the world through social media, which is often seen as its own superficial bubble.

My '60-second sermons', as they became known, are often inspired by quotes, stories, and lessons from Christianity and the Bible and, through them, I share my thoughts and try to uplift others in their day-to-day lives. 60-second sermons are not big, in-depth theological discussions, and I think that is part of their appeal. In them, I aim to talk about faith and God in an approachable, accessible and, hopefully, inspiring way. I want to tell people that they are loved, and to spread a message of positivity online that helps people to lead fuller lives offline, too.

Each chapter in this book begins with a 60-second sermon. It sets the tone for the chapter that follows, and is a digestible thought to take with you and think on as you read. This book is also made up of stories from my life, and my thoughts on the lessons in faith than can be learned from moments of hardship, sadness and joy. I am by no means perfect – I still get things wrong sometimes and I make mistakes; I sin, I stumble, I fall – but I hope that, just like with my 60-second sermons on Instagram, you can take a message of light, love, forgiveness and hope from these pages, and lead a fuller life, filled with kindness and hope.

Bless you, you're loved.

A NOTE ON THE GOD POD

I believe that God is everywhere, at all times, in and throughout his creation, which is to say that he is able to speak to us through all things; all God requires is for us to listen out for him. I often connect with God and my faith through art, whether that be a painting, music or a film. It doesn't have to be particularly religious – often it can help if it isn't, as my personal interpretation and response to it makes the sense of connection all the more special. Often a song comes on the radio which affects me in a deeper way than the others before or after it. It's as if God has dipped the music or lyrics in his spirit and sent them flying into my soul. In just a few seconds it can shake me awake and give me a profound sense of being heard and also spoken to. Sometimes I listen to music with a 'God filter', meaning I listen out for moments when God speaks to me through the words of the song.

So I thought it would be fun to give every chapter a kind of theme tune, and let you in on some of the songs that particularly resonated with me as I wrote this book and thought on what it means to live a full life. I've chosen songs that I have personally felt the presence of God through, and each one is in some way related to their respective chapter. In what is probably an act of nostalgia for my old (and now sadly defunct) iPod, I call it my God Pod Playlist! Interpret the songs on this spiritual soundtrack however you wish – a sense of something bigger than you, of being connected to the universe or however you prefer to think about it – but for me these songs feel like they create moments when God puts an arm around us, or reminds us he's here with us, or gives us a sort of spiritual high-five to uplift and re-energise us! I hope you enjoy the music and the chapters that follow.

CONTENTS

INTRODUCTION

While I was training to become a priest, I lived in Africa for a time. The continent forms a bedrock of my faith as so many memorable things happened there. In Zanzibar, where I spent my first-ever Christmas away from my family, I stayed at a Rastafarian-run guesthouse that consisted of a few huts on stilts on the beach. Aside from me, the guests included a Buddhist and a Muslim. Together with the Rastafarian, we sat by a fire on the beach under the Milky Way and discussed the divine. It was a magical evening and one where I learned a great deal, as we respectfully listened to one another and swapped stories, like travellers of old meeting on the Spice Trail.

Many of the insights gathered in this book borrow from my own experiences and the Bible, and I make references to and draw upon atheists, poets, people of faith and pre-Christian thinkers alike. In the chapters that follow, we'll explore death, grief, self-worth and identity; mental health and finding stillness in ourselves – however noisy the world around us may be – as well as learning how to forgive, seeing ourselves in a more positive light, improving relationships, practising positivity and finding our calling and purpose.

Working as a missionary in Tanzania, just after I had been ordained in the Diocese of Mount Kilimanjaro, I was asked to baptise a baby who was just a few hours old. I remember my sense of awe and privilege at my new 'job'. The baby and mum were still inside their *banda*, a low-ceilinged mud hut which is accessed through a single entrance and loops back into itself like a spiralling seashell. It was dark, warm and musty, lit only by the glowing embers of a dying fire on the floor in the middle of the room. My eyes needed a few moments to adjust, as I had just stepped out of the blazing sun. To one side of the room was the bed, made of sticks and mud and carefully laid with cowhide. The mother lay upon it holding her tiny baby. I was given a small metal bowl with water in it, and she gently placed the baby in my arms. The baby had not yet been outside, nor seen the sky or felt the sun, but there and then I prayed for the mother and baby and pronounced the words, 'In the name of the Father and of the Son, and of the Holy Spirit.' It was quite amazing. I have baptised hundreds of children and everyone is special, but I will always remember this one.

My spiritual formation was founded in Tanzania, and with it a sense of being connected with everything around me. Here in the developed world we may have more materially – better healthcare, transport, technology and education – but for all of this we are less *connected* with each other and with nature. People need some kind of spiritual scaffolding to support them, a structure to help them uncover the mysteries of life and an assurance that they are not here by accident, and nor are they alone. The large following I have on Instagram – which still baffles me – allows me to channel my faith and spread warmth and, I hope, understanding into the cyber world, a place that can often be superficial and cruel.

With each new generation, our societies are encouraged towards greater free-thinking and questioning of the status quo; we are increasingly prepared to challenge historic complacency towards our treatment of the planet, and widen our understanding of race and the iniquity of unconscious bias (as we've seen with the Black Lives Matter protests). I can understand that some might regard the traditional church as a little 'last century', but the message of God is timeless – and whether or not you believe in him, I want to articulate to you that you are loved and valued by him.

According to the Mental Health Foundation, one in six adults in the UK suffers from symptoms of mental ill-health, like anxiety or depression. Twenty per cent of us have thought about suicide, and of those in the UK who are receiving unemployment benefits, a shocking 43 per cent have attempted suicide and 33 per cent have self-harmed.

The main sickness of our day is identity. People don't realise that being *themselves* – being a creative human – is enough; they have an inherent value, they are loved and they are *worthy* of love. The world wrongly says, 'You are what you do, what people say you are, and what you own.' That just isn't true, and for those who live their life believing that these are the only measures of worth, their inner well-being ends up being as dry and lifeless as the Sinai desert; it's a seemingly one-way ride to a very empty cul-de-sac of materialist things which quickly lose their appeal once acquired. If you're at peace with yourself and enjoy what you're doing, you are far more successful and wealthy within yourself than billionaires who spend empty money chasing material assets but still find themselves wanting and lost.

Social media can be a useful communication tool, but unfortunately it is misguidedly used for self-promotion by many who create a fantasy to mask the reality of their lives. For example, on Instagram, when people say 'Look at me and my perfect life!' through the pictures they post. Like an actor who blurs the line between the role they are inhabiting and their own self, many people try to live up to the heightened version of themselves that they are projecting online, only to then wonder why they no longer know who they are. It's easy to get lost in the sequins and filters of fantasy, but beneath this thin veneer is a quagmire that will suck you down.

Twitter and Facebook, when they first started up, were supposed to generate an online community of encouragement, helping people to connect and share ideas, and in many instances this has been the case. Think how they enabled communication during the Arab Spring in places like Iran, and aided the organisation of impromptu environmental marches and, most recently, peaceful protests for the Black Lives Matter movement. And yet there are many cases of these social media platforms being dark ravenous places in which to pull others down.

My own intention on social media is to draw the attention away from myself and direct people towards a better, more satisfying way of living. To ultimately communicate to people that they are loved, whether they are airbrushed to perfection or just themselves.

At the time I began writing this book, in early 2020, Covid-19 had us in its infectious grasp and the world was beset with fear and anxiety. Even my church – like all religious buildings in the UK, including synagogues and mosques – was mandatorily closed to its parishioners; something that hadn't happened in Britain for around 800 years. TV news showed us a constant stream of ominous predictions and deathly data; it felt like a moment when I really needed to feel connected with God, and an incredibly relevant time to be writing this book. That said, if by chance you're reading this in the future, I'm sure – although I hope I'm wrong – that the earth is probably still beset by fear, paranoia and self-doubt; all symptoms of our brokenness.

I hope you will find sufficient wisdom in these pages to make your life and your soul both fuller and more resilient to the unpredictable times we live in.

Chapter One

Facing Goliaths

In the Bible, David defeated Goliath by trusting in God and in his grace. He couldn't have done it alone. We all have Goliaths in our lives, those big giants that seek to dominate and control us, or act as a troubling shadow in the background, casting their darkness and imposing their will over us. They often fill us with fear, worry, anxiety, trepidation . . . basically all bad stuff. I want to encourage you to realise that, however big your Goliath feels, hope and faith are always bigger. Remember, David overcame his nemesis, and so can you. You are not alone. Know that you are loved.

God Pod Playlist, Track 1: 'You Don't Know Me' – Armand Van Helden

This song is all about addressing the criticism and negative voices that can judge us and bring us down. The lyrics really speak to me, and this song feels like a big 'up yours' to the Devil, or however you understand him, and gives a great sense of taking back control of your life!

The Bible tells the tale of when the Philistines met the Israelites in battle. Their champion was the unassailable, nine-foot-tall Goliath, while the Israelites had little David, a shepherd. He was the only one of them brave enough to go up against the human monster.

The two armies faced one another on opposite sides of a gorge, but neither wanted to expose themselves by advancing across the valley, so Goliath began to taunt the Israelites. 'Let's do this the traditional way,' he roared, 'your champion against our champion.' Day after day he mocked them. Finally, David said, 'Why are we letting him talk to us like this, insulting our God? I will beat him.' Rejecting King Saul's shield and armour, which were too heavy for him, David chose to use his simple sling and stone, with which he had confidently defended his flock in the past against wolves and bears.

One of the first lessons you should take away from the story of David is not to focus on that which you're lacking, but instead focus on what you *can* do – the resources that you already have – to help you face your giant. For David it was his belief in God, but it was also his belief in himself.

Sometimes in life we face seemingly insurmountable problems: Goliaths, if you will. These come in all shapes and sizes. On a human level they may take the form of addiction, crippling self-doubt, panic attacks, illness or abuse. On a much vaster scale, we recognise them as poverty, war, injustice, and other societal failings that feel impossible for one person to fix on their own. What all these Goliaths have in common is fear: fear of failure, fear of dying, fear of being alone, fear of the unknown; the kind of fear and paralysis we experience when we feel too small to make a difference – an existential fear that we will fail to fix the problems in the world.

Fear is truly an odd thing. It spreads like a dark sludge within us; we can feel it seep in our chests constricting our breath, or weighing down our arms and legs with fatigue. Curiously, 'Don't be afraid' is God's most common phrase in the Bible. Fear can pin us frozen to the spot, make us turn tail and run, or blindly fight. But fear also has its uses. Throughout humankind's existence, it has often kept us alive, thanks to our heightened warning system that steers us away from anything that could seriously harm us. And yet, sometimes, this warning system can be a little outdated and overly cautious. For while fear needs to be acknowledged, it shouldn't always have the final say.

While caution can be helpful if we're wandering down dark alleyways in an unknown city after sunset, fear that focuses on all the bad things that *might* go wrong as soon as we step outside our front door is negative, limiting and ultimately unhealthy. For just as we grow when we face our fears, we lose a little part of ourselves each time we turn and flee.

When I lived and worked in Tanzania, our mission house was located deep in the bush. There were no tarmac roads to reach it, little electricity, and our water was caught from the rains. At night you could hear the sly *whoop-whoop* of hyenas calling to each other. Hyenas are much bigger than you might think, especially spotted hyenas; they're incredibly strong and their jaws are among the most powerful in the animal kingdom.

The week leading up to my ordination to become a deacon in the church and enter holy orders, I decided I'd walk to a large, strangely shaped boulder that, thousands of years ago, must have rolled off the nearby mountain. Massive in size and oddly square, as if hand-carved by a giant, the boulder had a huge lightning-shaped crack through its middle where a tree had forced its way through.

The only way to climb the boulder, which was about twenty feet by twenty feet, was to enter it through this large crack and follow the path of the tree trunk – part of which stuck out from the boulder and into the sunlight to form a sort of ledge. The trunk had carved out a decent-sized route through the rock's centre that I could clamber up through to reach the top. The branches and foliage of the tree formed a natural canopy, sheltering the boulder like an umbrella. Every so often, I would sit on top of this rocky balcony, in the merciful shade, and pray. It was a hike to get there and then a tricky climb to reach the summit, but I resolved to make the trek and pray there the day before my ordination, leaving early in the morning in order to watch the sunrise.

A few days before my intended departure, the local police chief dropped by the mission house to alert us that a man had been killed by a hyena behind our school. Hyenas are scavengers by preference, but if they can't outnumber a leopard or lion and steal their fresh kill, they are more than prepared do their own hunting. Come nighttime, inebriated humans are easy targets. Tragically, it seemed a drunk Maasai man had dozed off in our village and the hyena had eaten him. A horrible death.

When I got up on the morning of my journey to the boulder-tree, it was still dark. As I began my hike, I could hear the hyena in the distance. Shortly, I came to a dried-up riverbed, which acted as a kind of boundary marker, and here I paused. By crossing it I was heading into rough bush terrain, entering a place I knew little about in the daytime let alone in the dark. There would be no one who could help me if I ran into trouble.

Behind me: the school, familiarity and safety. Ahead: the unknown and the hyena. Fear punched me in the gut and demanded: 'What are you doing – you could easily be killed and eaten! Seriously, what are you doing!?' My heart was racing, my mouth coppery, my mind clouded; everything inside me seemed to revolt at the prospect of being eaten, saying, 'Turn back!'

I stood, frozen.

Next, I tried to calm myself by reciting Psalm 23, which explores the ups and downs of life, the sense of freedom in green pastures, and the depths of terror in the shadow of death: 'The Lord is my shepherd, I shall not want . . . He leads me in paths of righteousness for his name's sake . . . He lays me down in green pastures and restores my soul, yea though I walk through the valley of the shadow of death I shall fear no evil . . .'

The first and hardest part of facing your Goliath is taking the first step. Gingerly, the night still painted upon the baobab trees, the shadows of dawn a way off, I put one foot forward on the dried riverbed, and then the other. An hour later I arrived at the base of the rock and began my ascent into the dark cavity. But something besides me was moving around in there, something big. For a few moments I wondered whether it was the hyena. As I emerged from the rocky crevice and onto a ledge, I heard a sudden cracking sound and, turning awkwardly in the tight space, I found myself eye-to-eye with a massive owl! I'd stumbled across its nest, where the tree had forced its way through the rock and to the fresh air of the ledge, and it now sat no more than three feet from me, angrily flapping its wings and screeching. Admittedly, I don't know much about owls, but this thing was colossal, about the size of my torso. I realised that in order to climb to my prayer balcony I had to pass this giant bird. As I crept closer, towards its sharp talons and beak, it flickered its amber eyes and launched itself off the ledge, gliding into the night.

And so finally I reached the summit, where I sat and witnessed the rising sun as it slowly poured its mellow light over the vast landscape, soundtracked by the calls of waking wild animals. Having faced my fear of the unknown – first the spectre of the hyena, and later the owl – I felt a sense of satisfaction within myself, and a sense of growth. It made the moment there all the more special, the view of the goldening bush something to be savoured. Maybe at this point I should say something along the lines of 'Don't try anything as reckless as this at home!' but I had felt I needed to do this for myself.

Whether you are worried about an exam, a bully or an unopened letter from your bank, by facing these things head-on we grow wiser and stronger from the experience. Although the world is still an imperfect place filled with various dangers, great and small, we shouldn't let the fear of the unknown and the what-ifs hold us back from experiencing the joyous, sunrise moments in our lives.

We learn more about ourselves through fear and the way we respond to it than we do in times of complacency. For me, the hyena was a kind of Goliath. As I stood upon that riverbed in the darkness, considering whether or not to leave the safety of the mission and venture into the bush, I heard him whooping in the distance. What if I ended up being the animal's breakfast? Fear coiled in my stomach like a serpent swollen with what-ifs, but as soon as I took the first step, my head cleared and the snake disappeared. My limbs felt full of purpose as I walked through the early-morning dark, and with each step courage grew within me.

When we face fear and look our monster in the eye, it is the monster that shrinks, not us. Focus on what you *can* do rather than what you can't. It's about being hopeful and positive.

Whether a country is a rich, developed nation or an impoverished one, fear visits all its citizens. As you watch or read the news, it's easy to feel small and worthless in the face of disasters, pandemics, political corruption and corporate skulduggery, but you must remember in dire times that you are more than what you feel right now, and who you are is not your current context. You are a phenomenon, and each and every one of you is unique, but far from being alone you are part of a chain, a garland of life which began with your forefathers.

Alternative modern-day preacher Mike Skinner of The Streets says in the song 'On the Edge of a Cliff' that every one of our ancestors looked after the following generation, who looked after the following generation, and so on and so forth, so that one day we could eventually be here. That's pretty special when you think about it.

We all carry a level of injury and brokenness in our being, and our thoughts naturally seem to gravitate towards self-sabotage. You see this acutely with people who suffer from addiction, but this brokenness is part of who all of us are and what makes us human; even in the greatest moment of joy there is a vein of incompleteness within us, just as in the depths of despair and pain there is a glimmer of hope and goodness. Christians believe that one day we will be brought to an eternal place of no suffering or pain, but we're not there yet, not in this life.

I once conducted a wedding for someone whose father had passed. You had this wonderful day and celebration, but everyone carried a sense of loss and wished that the father could be there. At funerals, there is great sadness because of the love that was felt for the person who has passed. In sadness there is joy.

There is real freedom in being able to accept your brokenness and yourself. Depression, mental illness and hardship attack who we are, convince us that we are weak and less than we actually are, but they can also bring with them the gifts of wisdom, humility and the renewal of our self-knowledge. As a Christian, I believe we are all of inherent value to the creator of all things, and he knows every hair on our head; he has known us since we were born into the world. In the midst of pain, holding on to that sense of truth is very powerful. That's why hope is such a treasured resource.

You don't need to believe in God to share in that thought, either. I once heard a scientist say something along the lines of: 'Even in pitch-blackness, the photons that make up light are still present because of the creation of them in the beginning. Even in darkness there is light.' That scientist understood that light is composed of electromagnetic energy created a quintillion (think a billion billions) years ago and, although these photons are invisible to the naked eye, on an atomic level – even when no visible light is present and we believe we are in darkness – we are always surrounded by light.

Sometimes we can know something with our mind but feel something different in our hearts. We can see that family members love us but yet we feel unlovable. We all, at times, feel sadness for whatever reason, but don't let that sadness infect your self-worth and make you forget your value. In turbulent times it is easy to feel emotionally overwhelmed, but you are not the sum of your emotions. The real you is deeper and stronger than that. How you feel at any one moment may seem a permanent state – but it's not, because things are always moving. For instance, when you're down you often think you're stuck like that, but really you're in constant flux, prey to the changing thoughts inside your head. And just like how the sun is hidden by storm clouds temporarily, the dark mood from those thoughts will eventually move on and your smile will return. It's okay to feel sad, but however much you might feel like this sadness is all that you are, the real you is not defined by these top-level emotions or whatever is on the surface. It lies somewhere much deeper within yourself.

There is a remarkably big oak tree in the park outside my house, which I can see from my window. It is hundreds of years old and sometimes I seek solace in its shade. This mighty oak reflects the season on the outside – the bareness of winter, the blossom of spring – but the true essence of this sturdy giant is its interior and roots, which go deep into the earth. Its strength lies in that which you cannot see, just as your strength is deep within you and always has been.

Thomas Keating, an American Cistercian monk, co-developed 'centering prayer'. This is a meditative way of seeking the presence of God and being close to him, not through active prayer but by stilling the mind, sitting peacefully, closing your eyes and choosing a sacred word to represent him. Each time thoughts, feelings, images or perceptions start to invade your quietude, you anchor yourself using your sacred word. Keating believed we settle into our thought patterns too easily, thinking we are only what our emotions tell us, and we accept the judgements about ourselves and the world that fill our minds – when, in fact, who we are and how precious we are is so much more than we know.

Just like photons, goodness can always be found in moments of darkness; we just have to focus on it and look for it. We also have to trust and believe that it is there. Our purpose needs to be stronger than our emotions if we are to fulfil our goals of helping others, as our ego will try to rein us in and keep us from doing anything that might threaten the status quo. Many saints have gone through extreme depression and been to hell and back (figuratively speaking!) in pursuit of understanding, and at times they had to put their emotions to one side so they could do God's work. St John of the Cross famously went through a very dark period in his life, which can now clearly be partly attributed to depression. He wrote a very moving poem called 'Dark Night of the Soul', where he talks about finding God in the darkness that surrounds us. His major comfort was knowing that God was still in there the dark, feeling his pain with him.

Recently, a decade on from my formative trip to Tanzania, I was conducting what was to be the last service before the Church of England issued the directive that churches were to close due to Covid-19. There was an amazing sense of intimacy – a vulnerability and a connectedness that we feel as humans when we experience dark times together. In moments like this we are reminded of our frailties, and we need faith – faith in ourselves, faith in God (if you are religious) and faith in our fellow man and woman.

Many of us are understandably full of anxiety as normality slides further away. President Franklin D. Roosevelt once said that we have nothing to fear but fear itself, meaning that blind unreasoned fear is our worst enemy, as it stops us in our tracks with its hysteria when instead we need to trust in ourselves and maintain hope. But Covid-19 is an unfair opponent as it's an enemy without a face, which makes it even more frightening.

The world is in a really odd place. We have to make sure a greater disease doesn't also spread – fear. The Bible says perfect love casts out fear. I want to encourage you to have hope and to pray. But even without being religious, we can all take a meditative moment to slow down, tune in to how we're feeling, and relax. Meditation invites the soul to stillness and calm, and is partly about controlled conscious breathing. It is a great way to check in on yourself through the signals your body is giving you. Where are your thoughts taking you? Are they making your heart beat quicker than it needs to?

When I was in Tanzania, a friend told me a story. He'd been driving in the deep bush one morning, miles from anywhere, when all of a sudden his tyre burst. There was no spare in the back, he was about an hour's drive from the nearest village (which meant a six-hour walk), he had just a small bottle of water with him, and the day was getting hotter with every passing minute. Added to which, there was no signal on his phone. He was in real trouble, and began to panic as he ran through his limited options . . . What on earth was he going to do?

As the hopelessness of his situation started to sink in, a Maasai tribesman appeared, followed by two more. Neither he nor they spoke the other's language, though from his worried expression and his best attempts to explain what had happened to his tyre, the tribesmen understood. They spoke a while between themselves, then took the car wheel off before disappearing back into the bush without a word. Twenty minutes later they returned, each of them carrying massive bundles of grass. My friend waited patiently as they took a knife to his inner tube, cutting it open and stuffing the tyre with grass, packing it so compactly he was able to drive on it for an hour to the next village, where he could call for help and find a more permanent fix for his problem.

There is usually an answer to most problems, and often it appears just as you are giving up hope. When we step away from an issue and get some distance between us and it, we see that the solution lies all around us. The key to unlocking the answer is about not holding on to control too tightly, but rather letting go and trusting in silence and stillness – which may better equip us to hear the whisper of God. Problems don't solve themselves, but sometimes we need to allow space and not force a solution, for it is then that the solution shows up.

A great way to resolve problems can be to remove yourself from the business of the modern world, and allow yourself to slow down in nature. My family and I are very lucky – we live next to a small park with a kids' playground, mature trees and a large patch of grass. From where I sit now, I can see that wonderful oak tree spreading its limbs high into the sky. It's so enormous it would take forever to climb. I like to go and sit beneath it when I need to unwind. It's as if just by sitting beneath it, it feeds my soul.

As I study those magnificent branches, I think how strong it looks and that it must have borne so many seasons, and endless frosts, diseases and storms. I think about its lifespan, the things it must have witnessed happening beneath it. Wherever you are, hopefully you have access to the soul-tonic of nature – flowers, branches, water. Whether or not we are religious, I think we can all find profundity and wonder in the world around us. We should seek it out and plug into it.

The world is constantly telling us what to do and think. Many of us live with a constant stream of white noise from the moment our alarm goes off in the morning: checking our social media over breakfast, climbing in the car and listening to the radio on the way to work, and yet more white noise at our desk. What we really need is to wake up to the day on *our* terms.

In Tanzania, the people of the bush awake with the dawn light, and sleep with the night as soon as it descends. There is a stillness there that we have lost in our busy modern lives; a connectedness to nature that comes through living life slowly. In order to truly be in the present – and with God's presence, if you're religious – all you need to do is slow down.

St Augustine was a brilliant man, but in his early life, like many men, he drank too much, suffered from lust and fathered a child out of wedlock. But then, following a profound encounter where he heard God speak to him in a child's voice, he surrendered his life to God and found the peace that had evaded him for so long. St Augustine wrote: 'Our hearts are restless, Lord, until we find our rest in you.' Each of us has a hole in us that we try to fill with money, power, sex or whatever else, but none of these things satisfies fully, for the hole is God-shaped and only he can fill it.

I believe some of the early church leaders and influencers – such as the 'desert fathers' and monastics – were among the first psychologists, given all their work in contemplation. A lot of cognitive processing comes from an early church leader, Evagrius, an early cognitive thinker who came up with the idea of listening to the voices of those that tempt us and understanding their tactics; hearing the way they speak to us and learning how to answer using the gospel. Try to listen to the voice of your fear, acknowledge it, and then answer it with a truth.

One of the greatest things a person can do is to ask for help. I myself saw a counsellor for a time, just to get my thoughts out and to have someone listen to me about my lack of headspace, which turned out to be a result of my willingly listening to so many others for so long at the expense of my own internal voice. During stressful periods at work, I sometimes felt my mind becoming overcrowded with so many thoughts that I struggled to get on top of them. It was really good to have the chance to get some distance from them and process everything with someone who would listen with kindness, patience and compassion. This admission may seem strange coming from a vicar, but although I do my utmost to support and care for my community, I don't have all the answers. There are many things I still struggle with, for we are all broken but we are all loved.

Perhaps you've already found the solution to beating your Goliath, or perhaps you haven't and it still haunts you. In this life we will meet many Goliaths, and it is the way we deal with them that dictates whether we are tormented by them or can be at peace with ourselves. Many of us meet our first Goliaths at school, in the form of bullies. A bully is, at heart, an insecure person who feels inadequate on the inside. If they were truly happy with themselves, they wouldn't need to pick on people weaker than them to feel better.

What happened to us in the past at the hands of a bully can often be burned into our psyche, and feel as if it took place yesterday. Really harmful experiences can become traumas – scabbed-over wounds that we help perpetuate every time we pick at them. Sometimes they are only fixable by revisiting, examining, and talking through them in therapy. If you have something that keeps poking its head up, it might be that you need to say or write down what happened and have someone hear you. Life is too short for you to carry around unnecessary burdens on your soul.

If you find yourself returning to incidents that occurred in the past and having the conversation you wish you'd had at the time, then you're still holding on to negative energy.

The good news is we have a superpower to hand that, unlike the Hulk's ability to be green and strong, is not temporally limited, and nor will its 'Flame on!' dwindle like that of the Human Torch. No matter how long ago a blow was dealt to you, this brilliant weapon can be activated whenever you wish, and its wellspring dwells in your heart. It's called forgiveness, and you'll learn about it in the next chapter.

Chapter Two

Learning Forgiveness

Whether or not you have faith, forgiveness is a superpower humans can wield, and it will strip any enemy of their power. To forgive others offers great rewards; and for the Christian it is not a request but a command. Forgiving someone is not easy, nor is it about accepting the pain another person, animal or agency has caused you. Far from it – it is a process where you can move from a place where an experience has power over you to a place you have power over it, so that it can no longer negatively influence your thoughts and actions.

God Pod Playlist, Track 2: 'Let Go' – Connie Constance

This song reminds me to let go of those who have hurt me, to let go of those experiences that are keeping me from being fully myself again; to speak to the pain and say, 'Enough. I am forgiving you, and it's time for you to let go of me and leave.'

Forgiveness has in it the fingerprint of the divine or superior being. When you truly forgive someone, your self-esteem grows. An unwillingness to forgive can lead to anger, bitterness and hatred. You can hear Yoda in the background, saying that fear is the path to the dark side and that fear leads to anger, anger leads to hate, and hate ultimately leads to suffering. And it really does, taking you to a twisted emotional state where nothing positive will emerge. We've all been around older people who possess grace and gentleness, those who have acquired wisdom over the course of their lives. But we've also met those who are still angry and bitter, living an unforgiving existence by feeding themselves repetitious negative stories they can't let go of.

Getting older should not be a curse. It should allow you greater and deeper perspective, and an existence in which you are enjoying the fruits of your earlier actions. If you try to live in a way which expresses and sows forgiveness, peace and joy, then those are the very same fruits that you will likely savour in turn. If you have only planted mean-spiritedness in the orchard of life, the fruit around you will taste bitter. You will always reap what you sow.

We are more powerful than we think, and we are capable of toxifying environments with our presence and our actions, just as we can ennoble and energise them. We should always be aware what we are bringing into a room or gathering.

I believe true forgiveness is not a one-off, it's a process. We can either choose to let go of the grudges and scars of things done unto us, or we can unintentionally feed their longevity by placing them inside glass cabinets in our memory, polishing them with our resentment. Sometimes forgiveness can feel a little counterintuitive, and while we might think that by bearing a grudge we are punishing the offender, it is really only ourselves we are robbing. When we perceive our abusers and bullies as monsters, we make them bigger. It is only by rehumanising them and releasing them with compassion that we can stop them injuring us. Until we forgive them, we are a slave to them.

We need to consider *why* they did what they did. What went wrong in their own lives that they felt so damaged they could only find their identity in damaging others? How insecure and small must they have felt inside, despite their apparent strength or outward size?

I remember at my school there was a bully. He was stronger and bigger than the other boys, and one day he pushed past me and knocked the crisps out of my hand. I decided I was going to teach him a lesson, so I said to my two friends, 'I'll start fighting him, then you guys jump in and help.' As can you probably guess, it was a flawed idea from the start!

Next thing I knew, he and I were fighting and he managed to get me in a headlock. At this point I could barely move or breathe, and I motioned to my friends to come and help – but, bless them, they just stood there, frozen to the spot. Now, the bully knew that I could handle myself and he didn't want to let me out of that head-lock for fear of what I would do in retaliation, so instead he just tightened his grip. The upshot is I almost passed out.

Following this encounter, I invested him with my fear – turning him into a monster I was now scared of too. I became increasingly terrified of him as I let the threat of him grow bigger in my mind and heart than it actually was. He was just a kid who'd become the way he was because he had his own 'stuff' happening to him: his father wasn't around, his home life wasn't happy, his mum was dealing with other things . . . I learned all this about him much later, and simply hearing about his own pain, from his perspective, rehumanised him in my eyes and made him appear as frail and vul-nerable as he really was.

It is possible to reverse human Goliaths from being monsters, once we see them through a lens of understanding and feel compas-sion for what they might be going through. Generally speaking, people aren't born evil; it's more nuanced than that. Understanding others *is* hard, but when we take the time to do so we can help our-selves process forgiveness, which ultimately makes us lighter and happier as people.

'Radical empathy' is a term for when you try to see things from another's perspective, stepping into their shoes and imagining how you might feel if you were living their life instead of yours. It's about really trying to understand their feelings and approaching them from a place of acceptance rather than a judgemental one. As Dostoyevsky wisely said, 'Nothing is easier than to denounce the evildoer, nothing is more difficult than to understand him.'

There's an American Indian story attributed to the Cherokee people, which says that we all have inside of us a black wolf and a white wolf. The black wolf is sustained by fear, anger, jealousy, greed, arrogance and hate, while the white wolf is sustained by peace, love, hope, compassion and courage. It is up to us which wolf we choose to feed at any given time.

To forgive those who have wronged us in the past is to say, 'I no longer acknowledge the hold you have had over me; I let you go, and with you goes my pain. Now I can carry on with my life.' Forgiveness is about taking the door off your prison cell.

Of course, you can't just sit there and say, 'I forgive you.' You need to process forgiveness; feel it in your gut and heart. Forgiveness is not a platitude, nor is it about telling that person, 'What you did to me is okay.' It's not about denying yourself justice, but rather acknowledging the wrong done to you and choosing to get past that and say, 'I am not going to hold hatred against you; instead I am choosing to release the burden you've caused me and I'm going to let it go.'

You may have to revisit this forgiveness a few times in order to really free yourself of the person that hurt you. Trauma caused by abuse and extreme bullying is at the very root of many addictions, and burrows deep into your psyche. You might be telling yourself you have no Goliaths in your past, but perhaps there are things you remember that still haunt you on your blue days or when you're feeling fragile. These are past Goliaths that need letting out of their cages; you needn't be their zookeeper any longer. Let that pain run to the shadows. It doesn't belong with you anymore.

The Christian teaching on forgiveness is that you have already been forgiven all the bad things you have done in your life and, with this knowledge, you should offer that forgiveness to others. If you've been abused by someone this is a very big ask of you, and you might rightly say, 'I've never done harm like that to anyone, why should I forgive them?' But until you forgive them, they will weigh you down and continue to torment you. Instead of allowing them to have a hold over you – a hold that can fuel your hatred and infect your values – you should address them head-on in your heart and tell them: 'I feel sorry for you, and I let you go.' There is no quicker way to depower a monster than looking it in the face and forgiving – or even pitying – it.

When I went to East Africa as a missionary, I knew that part of Jesus's teachings is to forgive. Forgiveness is a command, and we are trapped by not forgiving. As a Christian, I believe the ability to forgive is something that directly connects us to God, whose ultimate expression of compassion was to give his only son to mankind so that he could atone for our sins. The Bible tells us that Jesus Christ also forgave the robbers on the cross and even the men who were nailing him to it. Even if you don't believe in God, lightening your heart of old resentments and grudges can only make you a happier person.

I had an amazing experience in Tanzania when I was teaching some students to become pastors. At the time we were learning about mission, where we would visit villages and invite people to hear one of the students talk about God if they wanted to. We were discussing how to spread the gospel when one of the students, a boy called Noah from the Maasai tribe, said: 'Instead of *talking* about mission, let's go and *do* mission.'

I asked him where we should start, and Noah suggested the Ndorobo people, a traditional tribe who had curious practices, like hollowing out baobab trees so they could hide in them and fire poison arrows at passing prey. They lived in a very remote area, with no roads, no running water and no electricity.

But Noah knew how to reach them. We drove off-road, through bush, veld and forest. The tribespeople emerged when they heard us toot our horn. We preached and baptised that day and the next day, and just as we were leaving, a rolled-up swaddle of rags was thrust at us through the Land Rover's open window. As we drove away, we unwrapped the bundle to find a baby. A nurse was with us, and their quick appraisal revealed it had severe malnutrition and malaria, and was barely clinging to life.

We sped back to the mission. The baby desperately needed a blood transfusion, but for the transfusion to work it had to be exactly the right blood match, and the newborn possessed a very rare blood type. Its odds of survival dwindled further.

Wasting no time, we asked for volunteers. Noah was the first to offer his blood, and miraculously, he had exactly the right kind. 'How come you have the same type?' we asked incredulously. Noah smiled and explained that his father, now long dead, was actually of the Ndorobo tribe, not the Maasai. Noah's father had prospered as a farmer but was poisoned by other Ndorobo tribe members because they were jealous of his success. Noah's mother had spirited him to safety and they were taken in by the Maasai, who adopted Noah as one of their own. This had been Noah's first return to his old tribe since he was a baby; and here he was, giving his own blood to save a baby of theirs.

It was pure forgiveness. There is nothing else so Godlike in this world as the ability to forgive.

Chapter Three

Community

We are made for community. We thrive when we are surrounded by healthy, caring relationships, and God's plan was for all of us to ideally be born into loving family units, though in reality this is not always the case for everyone. The language of our communities should be love, and the best way to learn it is by being surrounded by people who speak that language. Community can affect every part of you: the way you see, feel and understand things. A good community is one that is confident in itself rather than fearful, and whose members seek to serve, be selfless and encourage one another. When done right, a strong and flourishing community is a taste of heaven on earth.

God Pod Playlist, Track 3: 'Baba O'Riley' – The Who

As each instrument joins in and the music starts to layer and build, I get a really triumphant sense of everything coming together in this wonderful mix of sound. To me this song feels like community, like it gathers the ingredients that give us all our ups and downs together and makes a beautiful pie from it. I want to eat it!

Community is an essential part of our personal growth. We learn about our weaknesses by trying to understand more about the weaknesses of others, just as we can benefit by learning from others' mistakes and their wisdom. In a community, there are things your fellows do which will sometimes irritate you, and that's only natural – like a neighbour who does DIY late into the evening, or never returns the favour of putting your bins out for collection when you're away, even though you do it for them. The positive outcome from this irritation is it then makes you wonder what you might be doing that annoys the other person! It's only from this empathetic place that you can learn grace and grow in compassion. And, if you have a genuinely unpleasant neighbour, rather than reacting to them on their level, consider what has made them end up this way and find mercy within yourself.

Community will at times produce greater pain as you allow people into your heart that little bit more, but it will also allow deeper laughter and joy. The lows are lower, but the highs are higher! Just as the Maasai Mara thirsts for the rainy season in order to bloom and sustain its wildlife, true community needs laughter, shared mealtimes, trust and kindness. When working together towards a common goal, we are at our best. Eat, pray, laugh and work.

'Love thy neighbour' means caring about the person next to you, and being willing to make sacrifices for them and go the extra mile. Rather than thinking, 'If I do this for them, I will get this back,' it should be a willing investment of your time for which you expect nothing in return. When you're helpful to someone it produces connection, which is the very heart of community, so instead of being insular and ignoring the chance to meet the people who cross your path in any given day, try to connect more intimately with them. It is only by connecting that we evolve as people. Nobody is an island.

Making a little adjustment can go a long way. I was once in a McDonald's ordering some food, and I read the employee's name-tag and said, 'Hi John, can I have a Big Mac, please?' He later wrote online: 'Rev Chris is the only customer who ever used my name. It felt really good.' I didn't see him as just a faceless stranger shovelling fries into a bag. We are not numbers; we are organic, breathing creatures capable of love, compassion and empathy.

Always arm yourself with a smile, be curious of others and encourage them to be their best selves. Think of something nice to say to anyone you encounter. Our society can feel like a desert full of isolated people. Perhaps, as you've all gotten older, some of your friends have started to drift further and further away as life takes them in different directions. Maybe you are an economic migrant who has moved to a new city for work, away from your family and old network of friends. In big cities especially, it is easy to get lost in the crowd. So put yourself out there and join a club – maybe it's for dancing, running, pottery . . . whatever it is, it will take a little courage as you push yourself out of your comfort zone, but I promise it will be worth it.

Comfort zones are not always that comfortable, anyway. They're just places of habit we idle in because we feel safe there. But safe is not sound; safe can be limiting and safe can hold you back. Think of the saints, the freethinkers, the eccentrics, the outsiders, the adventurers who suffered through great danger, pain or torture as recompense for not playing it safe. They may have experienced those hardships, but they followed their calling and blazed a fresh trail for the rest of us to follow. In many a great life, there are risks that have been taken to raise it above the norm.

Not that we should define a person's worth by how many big risks they have taken. Sometimes it can feel like a risk just to do something that goes against other people's expectations of you, or to choose not to do something your friends are doing. It can even feel like a risk to be your own person, as it can mean you find yourself going against the flow, but it's important to live your life in a way that feels authentically you.

We tend to gravitate towards our own demographic because it's easier, safer and more predictable, yet community and connection are often found more deeply across boundaries and when there's no common denominator. One of the greatest lessons I learned was when I was the chaplain to a homeless ministry. For three years I got to know many of those sleeping rough in London; I met people from such a diverse pool of human experience and built up real relationships with many of them. Jesus walked among the sick, the poor, the criminals and prostitutes; he saw nobody as beneath him or beyond his care.

There's something quite profound about finding connections with others from very different social backgrounds. Think how much we can learn from one another, and how much more colourful and diverse our life experience becomes when we embrace that which is outside of our usual social sphere. At my church, St Saviour's, we have this thing called the Community Café. At first we called it the 'Older People's Tea Party', but as many elderlies don't like accepting that they're older, we renamed it Community Café! The idea behind the café was to bring together people in our community who might otherwise not normally meet. Church should be a place where the usual demographic 'tribes' are ignored and new friendships can be forged across the generations. We have some amazing older people in our area with whom many of our younger churchgoers love to hang out. Many are amazing people of prayer and wisdom, and have lived fascinating lives full of travel with plenty of exciting stories to tell. Sadly, dementia has gripped a few of the older people but warm and loving conversations in well-known locations, like our church, offer, I hope, some companionship and comfort.

*

Community has been shown to have tangible health benefits, too. The Roseto effect is probably not something you've heard of unless you work in cardiology. It refers to a phenomenon in which a community enjoys a massively reduced rate of heart disease, and takes its name from the town of Roseto, Pennsylvania, an immigrant Italian community that was found to have almost no heart attacks among its inhabitants between 1954 and 1961. Compared with neighbouring communities, this staunchly traditional town had an inexplicably low death rate from heart disease, even among men in the most at-risk age range of 55 to 64. At first, they thought it was down to the healthy olive oil the Italians in Roseto used in their food, but on closer examination it turned out that they were also cooking with lard and eating a lot of fried food – not to mention drinking and smoking with abandon.

When Dr Stewart Wolf, a researcher at the University of Oklahoma, looked into the way the community operated, he saw how close-knit and cohesive they were. In many ways, the town was like a big extended family: taking meals together, old and young; listening to one another and giving each other support and encouragement. All of this is food for the soul.

Dr Wolf concluded the reason the residents of Roseto had so few health problems was down to one thing only – that people were nourished and sustained by other people. When we are surrounded by a community, our sense of worth and our well-being blossom; conversely, when we lack a sense of community, we wither.

Meanwhile, in the Japanese region of Okinawa, the elderly population have the enviable label of being 'the happiest, healthiest and oldest people in the world'. Aside from their primarily plant-based diet and the regular exercise of agricultural work and fishing for food, one of the reasons for their longevity is their strong sense of community. These rural islands are mainly home to pensioners whose younger relatives have left the community to find work in parts of the country with better financial prospects. The side effect of this is that the older members of the community must work together. Apparently, Okinawans don't stress about money even though they live in one of the poorer areas of Japan. This is because they each have a safety net known as a *moai* – a group of roughly twenty close friends, who come together daily to talk and play games. Each person in the *moai* also contributes the equivalent of around forty pounds a month to a communal pot. If there's ever an emergency, anyone in the *moai* can take money out if they need to, which cuts financial anxiety levels right down – something most of us can only dream of.

When I lived in Tanzania, we'd visit remote tribes. Living in their *bandas* (mud and stick houses), these communities took great care of one another, and if someone happened to get sick, the whole village would soon know and be ready to help. If there was a dispute between individuals or families, they would gather and talk about it. Just like in Roseto, the identity of each person was integrally defined by the close-knit community in which they lived. There was a sort of unity and collective understanding, qualities that have become increasingly rare in modern societies. Many people – especially those who live in larger cities – don't invest much, if any, time in getting to know their neighbours. It's common for British commuters to sit and stare past the person opposite them, careful not to make eye contact because to do so would be deemed 'weird'.

But, as human beings, we are made for community.

People thought that cinema might die out with the rise of things like Netflix, but the opposite has happened. Apparently cinema attendance has increased over the past few years and is now higher than ever, and I was surprised to learn that there were around 177 million cinema admissions in 2018, the highest it's been for almost twenty years. Statistics aside, I reckon it's because of that sense of a shared experience; we love feeling part of something bigger than ourselves. Online gaming has also grown enormously over the last decade, allowing friends separated by great distances to play together for hours.

Finding real and genuine ways to connect online is something we all search for. On Instagram, I share thoughts and encouragement with hundreds of thousands of people, and they share some of theirs with me in return. And I am still discovering what it means to have a sense of community online. For instance, when churches shut their doors in an effort to curb the spread of Covid-19, many Christian communities invested significant energy in setting up online services that their congregations can access online, allowing people to connect and to worship from the relative safety of their homes. During lockdown, my church community started meeting online via Zoom. Although we were all physically distant from one another, we actually found that everything felt much more relaxed and there was an even greater sense of connection as our parishioners chatted to each other from their homes, bedrooms and kitchens. Instead of putting on their social armour and walking into church, they sat comfortably at home, talked, prayed and sang together. It felt much more personal and intimate, and it was more like talking with a family member then a church acquaintance. This was a real and very welcome surprise to me.

When it comes to the internet, I feel like we are all toddlers with a new toy – and, while we love it, we're not yet able to use it correctly. Back in 1999, the late David Bowie referred to the internet as 'an alien life form', whose potential to do good and bad for society was 'unimaginable'.

Wisdom is found not in seeking division, segregation and tribalism because you have different beliefs, but by compassionately seeking genuine truth and being open to be taught by another, even when you hold very different convictions. When we recognise the true, beautiful humanity in one another, everyone is bettered and community is formed.

Chapter Four

Finding Your Calling

Recently, I've been thinking about calling, or purpose. I believe that God knows all of us, that he knew us before the beginning of time; that he knit each of us together in our mother's womb and he has a calling and purpose for every one of us. One of the things that sometimes gets lost when we think about calling or purpose is that you are more important than your calling, and your value is not determined by whether you succeed, fulfil or even find your calling. There are signposts to your calling in life – things that give you joy, things that give you life – but just remember, you have more value than the purpose that is set for you. Bless you.

God Pod Playlist, Track 4a: 'Hounds of Love' – The Futureheads

The song gives a sense of urgency and a desire for something that seems achievable but is still a little out of reach, and communicates the frustration of not always knowing the right way to go.

God Pod Playlist, Track 4b: 'Thunder' – Imagine Dragons

I feel this is like discovering your calling after courageously pursuing it, and that moment feels like thunder!

Having a calling is not confined to becoming a priest. A calling is when a person feels particularly drawn to something, whether that's caring for others, upholding justice, helping those less fortunate, teaching others new things, protecting the planet or dreaming up new ideas and inventions. Mine, it seems, was to live a life in direct service to God, which for me was best expressed as becoming a priest in the church and becoming a leader in my local religious community. My twin brother's calling steered him towards a different kind of leadership, and since joining the armed forces he's led men and women into and out of danger in order to help fight oppressive forces that harm their people. Becoming a soldier felt like the best fit for him.

A calling can also be outside the realm of paid professions, and there is value and beauty in doing something well – for instance having a calling to volunteer, care for animals, or to become a parent. A calling and purpose can go hand in hand, but if you miss your calling it does not mean your life is without purpose.

If you're older and reading this, or circumstances seem too difficult for you to follow your true path, please don't think your calling has passed you by. It is never too late to step into the shoes that were tailored especially for you. You may discover it at any point in your life, young or old, because it's always been there – whether it's becoming an artist, setting up a business or sailing around the world. Our inner wisdom, once we get in touch with it, reveals to us what makes us tick.

I've always been able to speak in front of people and be myself, while others find even the idea of public speaking terrifying. Your calling is often a broad and fluid thing. You may be called to be a teacher, but that doesn't just mean you'll be sitting in a classroom teaching children to spell, as it may be that your gift is more broadly to help people, not just children, understand and engage with new or difficult ideas. In the church we talk about the calling to the priesthood as a vocation, and the word 'vocation' has the same etymological root as 'voice'. So, in a way, your vocation is your voice; what you have to say to the world. Finding your voice is broader than acquiring a job title, so don't limit yourself or what you understand to be your calling to a mere category. Our calling comes from deep within us; it is a heart matter and, when we find it, it gives us a pure sense of joy as if we are at peace with ourselves. This conviction doesn't disappear on the breeze but rather emanates from within us and radiates outwardly. As the lobster grows, it cracks and breaks its shell as it expands from within. Eventually the shell falls off. When we are stepping out of our old ways and following a calling, we are tender and fragile like the lobster whose new shell has yet to harden. Callings can erupt from within us, and break apart the status quo of our previous life.

Joseph Campbell, author of *The Hero with a Thousand Faces*, sagely said that we should follow our bliss. When you follow your bliss – or calling, or purpose – you put yourself on a path that has been there all the time waiting for you, and suddenly the life you ought to be living is the one you are living. When your calling finds you, you'll likely experience a shift of gears in yourself, and a clearer focus and sense of direction. It's like a special 'power-up' in a video game; you will feel more energised in your body, more confident in yourself, and positive things will happen with more frequency . . . doors of opportunity seem like they're opening more easily.

Feeling thrilled about what you do is a blessing and an indication that you've discerned your calling – but it's not a guarantee. For instance, I get enjoyment racing around a track in a go-kart, but I'm not called to Formula 1! Likewise, you may be very skilful at something, but just being naturally talented at it doesn't mean you're *meant* to do it.

There will, every now and then, be crossroads in your life that you should recognise as an opportunity for you to listen out for your calling. It won't be straightforward, and you may have to make what appear to be sacrifices to access your true purpose, but as time unfolds you will see that what appeared at first to have been a sacrifice was just a necessary step towards fulfilment and happiness on a greater level. I had to quit a job and move to a different continent to realise I was meant for something greater.

Reaching out to others and letting them know that God believes in and loves every one of them is my sense of purpose, and the reason I jump out of bed in the morning (so to speak!). If you don't know what your calling is yet, perhaps you are not finding sufficient stillness in yourself to listen to your inner voice. Only through stillness can we really get to know ourselves.

The doctors, nurses and other frontline health workers across the globe who have worked tirelessly to save lives during the Covid-19 pandemic have done so despite their personal fears, fatigue and a shortage of adequate personal protection equipment – because their calling to care for the sick and vulnerable is bigger than themselves. Our callings may take us into the fire and place us in the way of incredible challenges, but it is in the flames where we meet our true selves.

The blossoming of a calling is that rare feeling of being in sync with your true purpose; that which you were born to do. I believe we all have a purpose in our life, if we listen out for it.

Do you remember what your hopes and dreams were as a child, before you grew up and were told to 'get real'? Perhaps that message was communicated to you unconsciously, by the society around you. Or maybe those dreams were crushed unintentionally by an overprotective parent or family member, who spoke without thinking. Most of us are so busy trying to fit in with what society and our friends and family expect of us that we neglect to listen to our inner selves, who often naturally know where we want to go. But before you learned to censor your imagination, what did you hope to accomplish in your life?

I was raised on what I call life's 'middle-class conveyor belt'. Born into a good family, educated at private school, I experienced all the predictable and relatively privileged things that usually follow. However, at twenty-one years old I wasn't happy with my life. I didn't know what I *really* wanted to do with myself and my family were worried about my lack of direction. But first, let's rewind a few years and give their worries some context. It's backstory time!

After school, I went off to Kingston University to do a Business Management degree. While I was there I met a nice Christian girl, but I also got in with the wrong crowd. We were into soft drugs like weed, and playing poker – the usual things many young guys do. There was a lot of 'banter' among us, and it was characteristic for the group to poke fun at each other, constantly. But I wasn't comfortable with that at all. In fact, I wasn't comfy in my own skin. I had no real idea who I was and kept asking myself, 'Is this it – is this all that life is going to be?' I was struggling to find an identity. It didn't help that, when my relationship ended and left me heartbroken and without an anchor, I returned to chasing after girls.

I completed my degree and was fortunate that my parents were able to help me buy a house. I got a job with a company who purchased land and built modular houses on it. I wore a suit, I drove a nice car, I had a comfortable life. But inside I was hurting, bored by my work and dogged by existential angst. I considered the career path ahead of me if I were to stay in that job. I asked myself: 'What if everything in the next ten to fifteen years goes really well with work? Let's say you end up running the company and have a six-figure salary – will you be happy then?'

I realised then that the answer was writ large inside of me in neon letters: *Absolutely not!* That was definitely not the life I wanted for myself, so I made the decision to step off that conveyor belt and walk a different path. It wasn't clear where this new path might lead me, but I followed it all the same. And that's when, for me, the real adventure began. Sometimes, the road less travelled is the one you should take. At the end of their lives, people tend to remember the opportunities they missed. The unknown is itself a kind of Goliath, and it's often a fear of the new that keeps us stuck where we are.

At around the same time as I was wondering what to do with my life, a good friend of mine dropped out of university. After-wards, his aunt asked him to come to Tanzania and help with a school and medical centre she was setting up with the church. 'After all,' she said, 'you're not doing anything, and I could use your help.'

He did just that, and once he was there he called me up, saying, 'Chris, you would love this place, it's right up your street.' He knew that I was open to adventures, but also that I had a level of faith and I was growing in it. So I put my house up for rent and quit my job. I emailed the bishop who was running the mission and told him that I wasn't sure what God was calling me to, but that I was thinking of coming out to help him in Tanzania. He replied that, as soon as I had a plane ticket, I should let him know my flight details and he would pick me up from the airport.

Everything was suddenly moving very quickly and fluidly, with one thing naturally leading me to another. But that's not to say it was an easy road. When my calling came, I had some nerves around quitting my job and leaving the predictable and safe world I'd been brought up to strive for. I was also going against all the expectations of my friends and family, which was hard, but I kept telling them: 'I need to find out who I am.' When you have a calling, opportunities will arise to help you on your way, but it still takes faith to overcome your fear of the unknown – to leave that comfort zone. Sadly, this fear is what stops many people from making big changes in their lives that might put them on track towards their real purpose. But my calling was so strong I had to listen to it.

The mission I was to live and work in was based in Tanzania, East Africa, in a very remote area three hours' drive into the bush and over nine hours' drive from the economic capital, Dar es Salaam. When I arrived at the mission, my faith instantly seemed to blossom. I taught English using the Bible because this was the only book that every child could get access to a copy of. It also made it easy for us to follow each other as we read through the text, with Swahili on one page and the English translation on the opposite side. I was constantly absorbing these wonderfully evocative Bible passages that really inspired me, and as months went by I could feel my intimacy and understanding of the book growing every day. Sometimes we'd visit church communities on what we called 'confirmation safaris'. I'd drive with the bishop through bushland for hours and hours on the 'dancing roads' – so named because cars jump all over the place on the unsealed surface. Over a long weekend the bishop would preach and baptise hundreds of people, then we'd head to the next location in the jeep and camp beneath that huge African sky peppered with stars.

Life in Tanzania and other areas of Africa is lived closer to the wire; in some places, if it doesn't rain the crops don't grow, and if it doesn't rain for long enough, people can't eat and the vulnerable die. I learned that many people in Tanzania are very open to the notion that there is a spiritual realm to life, and that they really engage with their faith and speak with God, which is both fascinating and inspiring. I have a photo of the day I was ordained. In it, I'm surrounded by my friends: Lazarus, Noah and Moses, who all kept a close protective eye on me. I felt like I had been adopted into their families.

My parents thought I might not return from Tanzania – or, if I did, it would be with a wife in tow. I suppose to them I was something of an anomaly; always unpredictable, they could never tell what I'd surprise them with next. When I rang my mum to tell her I had decided to become a priest, she wasn't surprised. In fact, she laughed and told me a story: 'When you were born, I went down to the chapel and prayed, "Lord, you gave me twins on Christmas Day and I feel like maybe there is a purpose in that, so I offer you one of them for your service."' She believed she had been blessed with an extra son to give back to the church and to God, and I guess that was me.

Usually there is some trajectory guiding us towards our purpose in life, a seed within us that over time grows and matures and gradually makes itself known. During our lifetime, forks in the road often appear before us, a big one being the choice of which profession to enter into. When a purpose begins to form it's like a celestial bearing – coordinates that are given to us which we feel deep within ourselves.

Thomas Becket experienced this strong inner stirring when he became the Archbishop of Canterbury, leaving behind the carousing days of women, wine and song he'd spent with his fellow hell-raiser, Henry II. His faith in God grew in tandem with the deterioration of his friendship with the King. Becket spoke out against the Crown's attempt to remove the power of the church and, after he was charged with treason, fled to France. Only the Pope's threat of excommunication persuaded Henry to allow Thomas back, and four of the King's knights took it upon themselves to murder Becket in the cathedral in support of their monarch. Becket's calling cost him his life, but earned him a sainthood.

When your calling comes, it may well lead you into the unknown – to somewhere dangerous and challenging you hadn't reckoned on – but it is where you're meant to be. Ultimately, when you're on your true path, it feels less like a choice and more like gravity drawing you towards that which you are meant to do. Becoming a priest felt less like choosing to do so, and more a gradual awareness that I was always meant to be one and it was a case of accepting this truth. It felt like, after years of not knowing who I was, I finally knew the real me. It was a calling from inside and outside of me. Choosing not to become a priest would have been to reject my true wish, and would have torn at my very being.

But even though I've found my overall calling as a priest, I am still discerning my calling within that role – and I am sometimes unsure of what that is, because, as a priest, I can send my energy off into a million and one different directions. Once you've found your calling, it's rarely as simple as 'I've found my calling, and that's that, I'm done now'. There is this constant process of listening to yourself, reassessing and adjusting as you change and move through life, so that you're always pursuing a path that feels most true to you.

We're only here on this earth once, so we may as well live a life that is truthful to who we are. Do you have a secret urge to do something different, or is there a place which seems to draw you in? To find your purpose, you need to keep your ears open for what your soul is whispering to you.

Don't let fear and habit grip you and make safe decisions for you. The tasks which we do are less important than the *way* in which we do them – that's to say, with passion and care versus being lacklustre and disengaged. When you are in flow and following your calling, you naturally put more effort and love into the way you go about your purpose.

Finding this purpose is different to fulfilling your potential. When you think about it, Jesus didn't fulfil his potential. In fact, his potential for power and greatness is what the devil used to tempt him, saying: 'Follow me and I'll give you the whole world.' Jesus could have had it all – fortune, power and authority – but instead he chose his purpose: to die on a cross for us. Sometimes finding your purpose may inhibit the realisation of your potential, but that's okay, because your purpose is more important than your potential.

When I was about twelve years old, a teacher wanted to set up a debate for my class around the question 'Does God exist?' One student took the argument against the existence of God, while I put myself forward to argue for his existence. It was the first time I'd ever debated and, as I wasn't a great student, my teacher was surprised by my zeal. Surprisingly, I won against a really intelligent kid. It's as if when we find our real strength and match it with what makes us happy – in my case engaging and connecting with other people combined with talking about God – everything else is just joining the dots.

When we look back for clues of someone's emergent calling, you can often find them from an early age. For instance, my school art projects were all about Christ. I even did a painting of me crucified, which sounds a little weird – but in my defence, I was studying Salvador Dalí and his relationship with religious imagery. In hindsight, I would say I had faith even back then, but I was not living it out, and nor did I have the relationship with God I have now.

Another signpost to my calling occurred on the day of my graduation from my first degree, when I was twenty. The ceremony was held at the Barbican, a large conference centre in the heart of London. This was at the time when I was feeling quite lost in life, and after the ceremony my parents and I walked aimlessly through the city. That afternoon reflected exactly where I was in life, drifting directionless and without a set of coordinates to follow. Then we rounded a corner and before us, with its twin towers and massive dome, St Paul's Cathedral suddenly loomed in to view. The original church building had stood upon the site of a temple to the Roman goddess Diana. In 604 AD King Aethelberht the First dedicated the first Christian Cathedral to St Paul. This burnt down and its replacement was later razed by Vikings in the tenth century. Many centuries later, after the great fire of London destroyed Old St Paul's Cathedral in 1666, the famous architect Christopher Wren was enlisted to redesign and build a new cathedral on the site. Wren's masterpiece was heavily bombed during the Blitz in the Second World War, with a bomb piercing its great dome and leaving the high altar in ruin. But still this magnificent symbol of British courage and the Anglican Church endured.

We decided to go in and look around. It was All Saints' Day and they were holding a communion service. I received communion and immediately felt lighter in myself, as if I was no longer drifting but had found my port. I sensed God saying to me: 'Okay, so now you've finished this chapter of your life, I'll be taking you forward – you will be working for me.'

It was in Tanzania where God really spoke to me and where I really listened. When I returned to the UK, I came back as an ordained minister, but I wanted to do more training and went to theological college. After I'd completed my further studies, I was offered a job in the Peterborough diocese, which had funded my initial studies at theological college. I struggled with whether I should accept it or not. The job did not feel like it was very me; it was an odd feeling. But I also knew that as a priest I was called to sacrifice, so perhaps I was meant to take it and let go of ideas about whether that particular job felt like a good fit for me. Wrestling with the decision, I prayed, and as I prayed an image came into my mind of hands held together in prayer. Early Christians adopted the palm to palm praying pose to show humility and that they were willing servants to God. They would assume this very humbling pose, as though bound at the wrist, freely and without any physical ties of bondage in a physical and symbolic show of devotion and servitude to God. But the hands I saw had no fingertips and, therefore, had no fingerprints. Fingerprints are unique and individual stamps for each of us, everyone's are different; intricate maps of whorls and arches that are ours and ours alone. As I debated whether or not to take the job in Peterborough, my vision of the praying hands without fingertips felt to me like was God saying that, although he was still calling me to be his servant, he did not want me to give over my identity entirely. That job didn't feel like me, and somehow I knew that the image I saw was meant to guide me in my choice. It was a moment of clarity; the message was 'Serve God, but don't lose who you are'. In the end, I turned down the Peterborough job. I believed that God was calling me to a priest role, but one that would better fit me and permit me to be person I truly am. I believed then that God had something different planned for me in London, and now I find myself in a wonderful place, as a priest in west London, where I feel I can serve God authentically as who I truly am.

My calling is unique to me. The way I went to Africa, became ordained and worked in different church settings – it all added to and enriched my purpose in life. But if I'm honest, I'm still discovering my calling in many ways. I believe that it is God's plan for me to connect with a younger audience on social media and spread his love. Along with being a pastor and setting up a new monastic order for young people called the Young Franciscans, I believe that communicating the love of God to everyone, and especially to younger people, is what I was put on this earth to do. All my projects, progress and achievements are developments of what God is calling me to do.

Frequently, people on their deathbeds say they wish they'd taken more chances in life, rather than played it safe. I say you're only here once, so when your calling comes be ready to embrace it. So many people are robbed of their calling because they are fearful and trapped inside a rigid system. I wish I could reach through these pages, take your hand and say, 'Have courage, my friend. You can step out of your stuck place and follow what is stirring inside you.'

People are like cars – only when there is movement can the steering work and change come. Money should not be the central aim of your calling. The happiest people I've ever met are not those who are rich but those who have found true expression through being honest with themselves and following that voice inside them.

The last thing to say on this subject is that we are of more value than our calling, and it should never claim 100 per cent of our energy. We all have family and friends who are part of our lives and need our time and love. At its most basic form, I believe our calling is to know we are loved and offer that love to those around us. Like a bird is born to fly, humans are created to be loved and to love; and, in this way, all of us are capable of finding love. We each have a calling that is unique and inhabits us. In order to find it, we have to be open, courageous, and prepared to gather momentum and try something new.

How do you know when you've found it? It will feel like coming home to yourself. Follow your bliss, my friends.

Chapter Five

Prayer

As humans, we are not made for an endless race; even the best marathon runners in the world still need rest and sleep. Likewise, our souls need stillness, and we need to slow down or stop every so often. More than chilling out and watching another series on Netflix, we need a deep silence. Contemplative prayer and meditation are two ways we can do this. Just five minutes of being still, allowing yourself to acknowledge being in the present moment: the floor under your feet, your breath entering and exiting your body, and being open to a loving God who longs for you to be with him. It is in this place we often find strength for the day and a peace that surpasses understanding.

God Pod Playlist, Track 5: 'Byegone' – Volcano Choir

It's hard to articulate the sensation that prayer can give you, but this song feels a little like coming into God's presence. Like being enveloped in love. Just imagine standing under a great crashing waterfall of love, drenching you through.

The Aramaic word for 'prayer' translates as 'having an openness to God'. I see prayer as a kind of spiritual nutrition; just as the body needs physical food to sustain it, so too does the soul need spiritual food. What is interesting to note is that all faiths have prayer at their centre; and, even in the secular world, prayer-like techniques like meditation and mindfulness are on the rise. As humans, we recognise prayer's importance. And approaching things with a prayerful attitude changes not only ourselves, but how we view and even impact the world around us.

As a Christian, I find that if I don't keep to my one-to-one prayers with God on a daily basis, I start to feel irritable and out of sorts. It's a relationship similar to that which I have with my wife; if we don't invest quality time in one another, we soon feel the distance grow between us. Personally, I need to be still with my God every day.

Prayer is the most natural thing in the world for us to do. It is by turns easy and hard. All of us have at some time in our lives made a prayer and appealed to some named or unnamed God –

often in a moment of crisis (for example, before an exam). A recent paper from the University of Copenhagen titled 'In Crisis, We Pray' stated that, during March 2020, as the Covid-19 pandemic began to hit Europe badly, internet searches on 'how to pray' skyrocketed. In April, the Church of England set up a call-in prayer line, and in the first forty-eight hours they received more than 6,000 calls. The *Guardian* also reported that, during lockdown, one in four people in the UK attended an online church service, which marked a huge increase in church participation.

I have found that the more we pray, the easier it becomes and the more we want to pray, because we experience the depth and richness of it. Learning to pray reminds me of meeting someone new: the introduction can be a bit awkward, but the more you speak to the person, the more comfortable you feel as you get used to them and their way of saying things, to the point that you eventually know each other so intimately that words are almost not even needed. The people who you are closest to in life are those you feel the most relaxed being in silence with, knowing their presence is there with yours. This sense of peace and equilibrium is similar to prayer – it's a place of relationship and stillness.

Many of us will have experienced little moments of clarity in prayer or meditation, and you may understand these moments of divinity and insight as epiphanies – instances when the world seems to make that much more sense than usual. Often, it's when you're immersed in nature and find yourself marvelling over creation's hand, like when you're watching sunlight pass through the filaments of a butterfly's wing, or listening to birdsong in a bluebell wood or the wind ruffling the green canopy of an enormous oak tree. We feel in these moments a stillness within ourselves that deeply connects us to the earth and creation.

'Epiphany' is from the Greek word meaning 'divine manifestation', and is also the name of a Christian season celebrating two events: the visit of the wise men to Jesus at his birth, and the baptism of Jesus by John the Baptist. Experiencing epiphanies and discovering greater depths in ourselves and the world around us is something we can achieve through prayer. When we discover the fingerprint of the divine in ourselves, when we recognise and acknowledge God's hand in other living things and have a sense of something greater than ourselves, something special occurs.

Prayer can be broken down into three simple categories. The first kind of prayer is the most common: it is a *personal* dialogue – a petition, if you will, to God, done through our heart and mind for ourselves and/or others. The second type is written or *liturgical* prayers, which we read out during a church service. These usually originate directly from scripture or are inspired by holy texts or hymns. And finally, there is *silent* prayer, which is more about sitting with God than speaking to him, enjoying his presence and allowing for communication without words. In the world today there's been a real surge of interest in inner wellness, meditation and the greater acknowledgement of a deeper spirituality. I think the world is changing, and people are beginning to see that being spiritually bankrupt but materially wealthy is no longer an option. Silence and stillness are one of the most profound ways to pray. In the Bible, Lamentations 3:26 and 3:28 tell us: 'It is good that one should wait quietly for the salvation of the Lord . . . it is good to sit alone in silence.'

You've probably all heard of mindfulness, which is defined as 'a mental state achieved by focusing one's awareness on the present moment, while calmly acknowledging and accepting one's feelings, thoughts, and bodily sensations'. I'd say mindfulness takes inspiration from Psalm 46: 'Be still, and know that I am God.' In other words, in your stillness you are knowing and known, being in the present with the presence of God.

The modern world is so noisy and invasive, and nor do we help ourselves much when it comes to finding inner peace. Your alarm goes off in the morning and wrenches you from sleep. You immediately look at the latest worrying news on your phone, and then move on to your social network feeds. You grab a quick breakfast and put the radio or TV on, then on the commute to work you've probably got earphones on, listening to music. Then, once at work, perhaps you put your computer on and go straight into 'task' mode. But at what point have you taken a breath and been sufficiently still, to remind yourself that you are an amazing, creative human being waking up to a fresh and beautiful day that is full of amazing possibilities? Meanwhile, the world tells you that you should buy this to look like that, and woe betide if you're fat, too tall or don't fit the mould in some other way. Remember that we are all miracles, and God loves us whatever we look like.

We need to slow down to our own natural speed, not force ourselves to keep to that which the modern world demands of us, for at a slower pace you notice more around you and can hear your inner self more clearly. The psychiatrist Carl Jung once said: 'Hurry is not of the devil. Hurry is the devil.' Being busy for the sake of being busy takes away the meditative rewards of rest and taking time out between tasks, and listening to ourselves and our bodies.

Certain religious sites, as well as natural spaces, lend themselves to prayer and meditation; these are places where our connection to our God feels clearer and more intimate. In Christianese we call this a 'thin place', where the boundary between the physical and spiritual is gossamer-like. Given that the world is noisy, aggressive and fast-paced, going to a place which is dedicated to stopping and slowing down – a sanctuary to prayer – is very helpful.

I have found these sanctuaries of stillness in many places, from the African bush to churches in busy cities. I remember a time when a friend of mine (who is also a vicar) invited me to go on retreat with him in the beautiful Welsh mountains. The retreat house there, Ffald-y-Brenin, is famous for the feeling of God's presence that is found there. As we drove to the house and parked outside, we were immediately aware of what felt like a father's love around us – and we hadn't even climbed out of the car. We didn't want to say or do anything other than just sit there and absorb this comforting feeling; the feeling of being gently hugged. So we sat in

God's presence for a while before we moved from the car and entered the building.

If you can find your own thin place to hear God's voice and to be heard by him, I encourage you to do so. Find somewhere quiet where you can think, and be still, breathe and bring to mind that God is present. It can be as simple as that.

I want to tell you a true story of how I once heard God speak to me – not in an impression, or through a feeling of peace, but an actual audible voice. It does sound weird and far-fetched, but all I can say is that it happened.

At the time I was living in Tanzania, and there was famine in my area. The rains had still not arrived, the crops were drying up, and people were either dying of starvation or severely ill with malnutrition. I was in church praying during a service when I felt a nudge from God to go and pray in my favourite thin place. I often climbed the mission's water tower and sat on its roof, like Spider-Man beneath the stars of New York. The views were amazing from up there, and it was the perfect chilled-out spot in which to pray.

Listening to God's command, I left the church and started walking towards the water tower, lazily thinking to myself, 'I don't really fancy the climb today. Perhaps I'll just sit at the base.' But when I reached the tower, there was a ladder leaning against it that had never been there before (nor did it ever appear again). For whatever reason, there it was. And since it would make the ascent much easier, I thought, 'Okay God, I'll climb up then.'

Sat on top of the tower, I started to pray. Nothing particularly inspiring – in fact I can't remember what I prayed for – but on finishing my prayers I suddenly felt yet another nudge to pray, but this time specifically for rain: 'Lord, please send rain.' No sooner had I said this than a clear voice above me, slightly to my left, replied, 'In three days.'

I opened my eyes to see where the voice had come from, but there was nothing there. It was weird how normal it felt to hear that reply out loud; no drum roll, no drama, I wasn't overcome by singing angels or suddenly bathed in a beam of light – I simply heard someone speak. Another odd thing was that, on hearing the voice, I felt cleansed by it and trusted it entirely; it was as if I knew it had never lied and could only speak truth. I felt comforted in my very being.

I told the students to leave their buckets out in three days' time because it was definitely going to rain. Definitely. They looked at me a little funny, but then I always was a little weird to them: the crazy *mzungu* (white person). I even told the bishop about the coming rain.

When Friday – the day of the rain – arrived, I was trying to complete a Bible exam but couldn't stop myself from repeatedly looking out of the window. It seemed impossible that it would rain. The sky was a perfect blue, without the merest hint of a cloud.

I silently addressed God: 'Lord, what is going on? I'm sure I heard you tell me it was going to rain and so I told everyone. Not only will I look stupid, but more importantly, my faith will be shaken because every bit of my being believed it was you who spoke to me up there on the water tower. Now this is the third day, so where is the rain?'

I felt the Lord telling me to have faith and patience, so I finished my exam and went to lunch. Halfway through lunch, a tinkle and then a musical ringing filled the air as fat raindrops fell upon the corrugated roof. *It couldn't be, could it?* Everyone jumped up and ran outside. It was pouring with rain! I sighed with relief and thanked God, then walked outside to join the others. Thick black clouds were stampeding across the heavens, so vast and dense yet they felt as if they had come from nowhere. As students ran about catching rainwater in brightly coloured buckets, one of them stopped, looked at me and smiled an impossibly broad grin before disappearing back into the crowd.

I love to pray, knowing that there is someone who cares and wants to hear me – who loves it when I stop and speak to him. Prayer at its base level is about being open and communing with God, not banging on his door demanding his attention. There is a mystery to the sovereignty of God and our freedom of choice: God's purpose will come about in the end, and yet we also have the freedom to reject or accept him. Does your brain hurt yet!? I think God longs for his creation to be open to his purposes and to be involved with bringing them to fruition, and a major way to be involved with God's plans on earth is to be a person who prays.

I believe we are enveloped by God, as is every living thing and part of creation – from the giant oak tree in the park beside our church, to the music I listen to. His spirit gives life to all things and he loves with an inexpressible love. His love is a fire and I want to burn brightly in it. And the best way to catch alight is to pray and spend time with him. Prayer is about gazing upon the beauty of God and in turn being in his gaze, for it is that which sets us aflame.

In *Finding Your Hidden Treasure: The Way of Silent Prayer*, Benignus O'Rourke quotes the medieval theologian Meister Eckhart, who compared coming to prayer with placing a damp log on a fire:

> In order that the wood may catch fire and be penetrated completely, time is needed, because the wood and the fire are so dissimilar. At first the fire warms the wood and makes it hot. Then the wood starts smoking and spitting and crackling, because the two are so dissimilar. But as the wood gets hotter it gets quieter. The more the wood gives up to the fire, the more peaceful it is, until at last it really turns to fire.

This quote from Eckhart fascinates me and makes so much sense. There's a dual reality in coming to prayer. In one sense it is really alien to us to sit and pray, like we are damp wood trying to catch a flame. It feels odd and separate to us, a strange other realm. But another truth is that prayer is part of who we are as humans; we are ultimately wood and we can join with the Father and burn easily. It takes some time to squeeze out the world and our own misjudgements, but when we do we discover this sacred dance of flame.

I love praying because it takes me into God's presence, where there is healing and wholeness. When my daughter Rose falls over and bumps her knee, she runs to my wife Jenny or to me to be embraced and spoken tenderly to. This helps her to get over the pain, and receive in its place love and security. Praying and being in God's presence is just like this, as we run to him in times of trouble and seek his embrace. And just as Jenny and I will hug Rose or our new baby Saoirse any time they want, likewise any of us can turn to God and seek his embrace at any time. He will not refuse us. He loves us with a consuming fire.

Like anything new, prayer takes practice; often while praying we are so busy trying not to think about other 'stuff' – a bill that needs to be paid; what someone said that upset us – while also trying to focus on being still, that we can't locate the peace and stillness we envisaged. Then we feel silly and discouraged for even thinking we'd get a response from God.

The answer is to stick with it, stay in the fire, remain silent and stay still.

If I don't pray in a day, I feel it. I miss it. If I'm surrounded by a situation that doesn't allow me to pray easily for more than one or two days, I start to experience a sense of grief. It's like a separation, not only from God, but also from myself.

Before Rose was born and I started my new job as the pastor of St Saviour's in West London, Jenny and I went for our last big holiday before we became parents: three weeks in Vietnam. In the north of the country, beyond the Perfume River, is a whimsically beautiful, geographically stunning place called Halong Bay. Looking like an illustration from a children's book, strange towering limestone karsts topped with trees and moss protrude raggedly from the green water of the sea. It's protected by UNESCO, and with good reason. It has an otherworldly aspect, and is like nothing I've ever seen on earth.

When we booked our trip on a traditional wooden sailing boat, we were unaware that what we were about to embark on was really a drink-all-you-can 'booze cruise'. While the other passengers were nice enough, these younger thrill-seeking party animals had a very different agenda (think nakedness and drunkenness!) to my wife and me. We just wanted to relax. Suffice to say, it was a tough trip, and while there were some fun times – like canoeing around caves – Jenny and I were really just trying to get through it. It was impossible to take ourselves out of the constant noise, and to be still and talk to God.

After the crazy boat trip, Jenny and I went even further north, to where the mountains of Vietnam meet China. Sapa is a market town, home to many ethnic tribes whose members wear bright traditional clothes and colourful headdresses threaded with silver jewellery and bells. Among them are the Hmong people, many of whom have experienced a Christian revival.

We arrived on a Sunday and went to church, but we couldn't get in because it was so packed. Instead, we sat outside, and as the Hmong started singing and praying, Jenny and I felt God's presence so powerfully that we both wept. We had felt starved of his presence those last few days on the boat; now, finally being in it, we felt refreshed and embraced. We could be ourselves again and let God minister to us, feeling his healing and nourishment.

During my time in East Africa, I took some time off my missionary work to relax and take an 'open water' scuba diving course in Zanzibar, off the coast of mainland Tanzania. First of all came the theory, for which I sat in a room and learned about the physics and physiology of diving. Then I practised in a swimming pool, learning how to operate the gear that would allow me to see, swim and keep breathing while underwater. Then came the final stage, the actual dive, for which I boarded a boat with a few others and went out to sea.

Getting into the water felt like falling over the side of the boat with a heavy backpack on. But, once immersed, I was utterly weightless. Using my buoyancy aid, I felt as if I were flying into another dimension. I loved it. It was like there was a whole other world under the sea. An underwater reef with its luminous seagrass and fantastically alien creatures – it felt like I was on a different planet. Hundreds of fish flitted around me and glided in and out of coral that looked as if it had been hand-sculpted and then painted in ghost-train fluorescents. It was exquisite.

Without goggles I would barely have seen anything; without the aqualung on my back, feeding air into my lungs through the regulator in my mouth, I wouldn't have been able to spend very much time under water. But with all the necessary kit, I was able to revel in this strange and wondrous environment, and I experienced a great sense of awe and wonder.

When we learn and practise prayer, we begin to sense, feel and see a whole new world around us, and it is every bit as bedazzling as what I saw that day under the waves.

When people think about prayer, they often fall into one of two camps. The first sees it as a means of accessing God's presence and living a life of peace and communion with him. The second sees prayer as something more intercessory: harnessing the resources of God for something or someone – perhaps for someone who is sick, to resolve a problem at work, or in search of a victory over some hurdle.

The simple truth is that the access-granting and resource-harnessing ideas are not mutually exclusive. Prayer is both about being with God, simply because he is beautiful and because in his presence we are embraced by love, and partnering with God to see his will done in our time on earth as it is in heaven. One of my heroes of the Christian faith is St Francis of Assisi, who really struggled with the question 'Should I become a mystic, retreat into a life of prayer and turn away from the world – or should I head into the world and preach?' He asked his closest friends to pray and ask God on his behalf. They all came back saying he was called to preach, even though all of his power and growth came from him being rooted in prayer. That's why Franciscans are friars and not

Above: Preaching at my church, St Saviour's in West London (left). When I arrived, I tried to foster an atmosphere of courage and faith, as well as a bit of risk-taking. This is around the time I began speaking to people on Instagram through my 60-second sermons (right), speaking love and light on social media and connecting with thousands of followers from around the world.

Working as a missionary in Tanzania. This photo is from the day I was ordained in the Diocese of Mount Kilimanjaro – a huge moment for me.

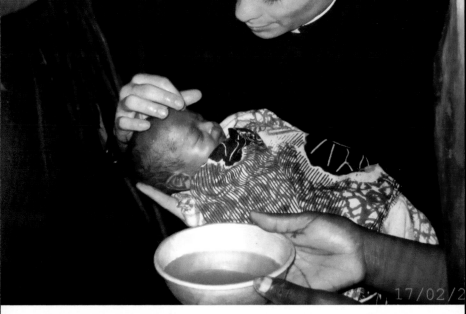

Above: Just after I had been ordained, I was asked to baptise a baby who was just a few hours old. I remember my sense of awe and privilege at my new 'job'. Since then, I have baptised hundreds of children and everyone is special, but I will always remember this one.

While I was living in Tanzania, the area was suffering from a severe drought. Crops were drying up, and people were either dying of starvation or severely ill with malnutrition. I prayed to God and asked for him to send rain. No sooner had I said the words than a clear voice above me, slightly to my left, replied, 'In three days.' I can't quite explain it but, on hearing the voice, I felt cleansed and comforted in my very being. Three days later, thick black clouds were stampeding across the heavens over our compound, so vast and dense yet they felt as if they had come from nowhere.

Above: Surrounded by my friends Moses, Lazarus and Noah. They were also training to become Pastors and they became my closest friends. We had a lot of laughs together, went hunting and camping, and they were with me when I got stung by a scorpion. Instead of sympathy, they just laughed and said, 'You're gonna be in sooo much pain, man'. Weirdly, that actually helped settle me – I figured that they wouldn't be laughing if I was going to die!

Below: At a Maasai gathering for young warriors in Tanzania. It was an incredible experience, and I tried my hardest to jump with the best of them.

Above: With my twin brother, Charles, i
our 'uniforms'. My calling led me to become
priest, whereas Charles' steered him toward
a different kind of leadership in the arme
forces.

Left: My brother and I were born o
Christmas Day 1982 in Dublin, Ireland
Years later, my mum told me that she fe
that maybe God had blessed her with twir
for a reason. She believed she had bee
blessed with an extra son to offer back t
the church and to God's service, and
guess – being a priest and all – that turne
out to be me!

Left: My family – my mum, two sisters, dad, and my twin brother. We don't usually dress up this fancy, I promise! My siblings and I are always challenging each other to do better while also rejoicing in the successes of one another. Even though we're close, we do still occasionally have our fallings-out – siblings usually do – but we never stop loving and appreciating each other. I'm immeasurably grateful for this.

It's a challenge to fit all of us in one selfie, but I did my best! Here is the whole family, on Christmas Day (which is also Charles' and my birthday), in my parents' home where I grew up. We're sitting around a huge walnut round table, a bit like the legendary King Arthur's at Camelot. All our family gatherings are held around that table, and it's the very heart of the house. Eating together is a necessary glue for strong bonds with our family, partner and friends.

Above and below right: Filming for the Jolly YouTube channel with Josh and Olly. This channel, along with their KoreanEnglishman channel, is where I first spoke on YouTube about faith. Appearing on these channels was the catalyst that threw me into the online world!

Below left: Hanging out at the beach with Jenny and two of my best friends, Andy and Sho (who you may recognise from the Jolly channel, too) They have a wonderfully curious mindset, and have the gift of making friends easily and putting people at ease by making them feel valued. I often say, 'To love well is to listen well', and they really are magnificent listeners. They are brilliant examples of 'humble confidence'.

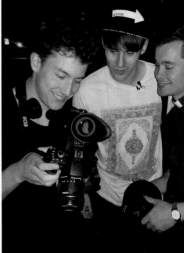

Above: In Cambridge, where I met Jenny. She said she started to fall in love with me on this bridge.

Right: On our wedding day. Jenny knows and loves me more than anyone else I've ever known. That is in part due to her knowing all my faults and loving me through them. When we first fell in love it was exciting but also terrifying, as I realised she could break my heart if she were to step away from my love and deny me hers.

Left: At home with Jenny, Rose (left) and Saoirse (right). Jenny and I try to go on dates once a week, where possible, doing things that we both enjoy. Sometimes we have spontaneous dance parties in our lounge, where we turn the music up loud and dance with each other. It's our thing and I know Jenny loves it. We work at our love, because its rewards are far beyond anything else this world can offer, and we help bring out the best in each other.

Below: A family day-out in Cornwall, the great domes of the Eden Project in the background. It was a sweltering hot day, but it was wonderful to take time out with Jenny and the girls – they're both growing so fast!

monks. Friars combine prayer with movement, whereas monks stay in the same place their whole lives and pray.

The great thing about prayer is that you can do it at any time and in any place (except, perhaps, on an accidental booze cruise in Vietnam), not just in churches. 'Extempore' prayer is the most common form, where people pray to God without notes or preparation and seek his help. Another method of prayer is moving towards what we call 'contemplation', which is less about *doing* and more about *knowing* and *being*. If extempore prayer in its simplest form is about speaking to God in a moment, then contemplative prayer is about looking at God and knowing he is looking back at you, acknowledging his presence and sitting with it. St Augustine of Hippo said, 'We come to God not by navigation but by love.' It is as we sit with the knowledge of God's love permeating through us that we can feel his embrace.

There are two types of silence that we experience: exterior and interior. Interior silence is not about the absence of noise, but about acknowledging the presence of God, present within you and behind everything. The psalm says 'Be still, and know that I am God'. Silence is the noise of God, and when he says 'be still' the psalmist is talking about an interior silence – though it can be helped by having an exterior silence, such as going to a quiet place. In order to find stillness, we must not battle but surrender, just like Eckhart's damp log submitting to the fire.

The practice of becoming 'still' is about acknowledging the thoughts that come into our minds and letting them go without engaging them. A method that helps me is to imagine my mind like a running stream in which thoughts are constantly moving, many of them fearful and negative. Often, we feel like a stone in the centre of the river, buffeted by the currents of these thoughts. And there are many of them – believe it or not, in any given day 70,000 to 100,000 thoughts cross our mind! What we need to do is to remove ourselves from this river of thoughts, and instead sit on the bank and watch the water go by.

In the contemplative method of prayer, a technique that some find helpful is centering prayer, which involves having a holy word or phrase that you say to draw your mind to a place of peace amid the chaos of your thoughts. Let me explain how to practise it . . .

Sit up straight on a seat, uncrossing your legs and arms so that the blood can easily flow around your body. The aim is to be alert and relaxed. Place your hands on your legs in a comfortable position, lightly resting them face down or turned upwards in an open gesture.

Take three long breaths, in through the nose and out through the mouth. On the last breath, purposely breathe slowly. Hopefully, you are now moving towards some sort of silence. It is at this point that your mind may start to wander, thinking about that difficult conversation you had or the email you need to send . . . or what you want to eat later. Whatever it is, say your chosen word or phrase. It could be 'love' or 'courage', 'light' or 'God loves me' – anything you feel comfortable with. Saying this word or phrase is like sounding a bell in your mind. It should not be shouted but gently spoken, like a feather resting upon cotton wool. This will draw you back to stillness.

Over time, it becomes easier to achieve and sustain stillness and you won't have to say your word so frequently. It is then that you will gaze at God and know he is gazing back at you. When we seek to become intentionally aware of God's presence, this is contemplation.

If contemplation is gazing at God, meditation is looking at something *with* God. The idea is to take a picture, thought or piece of scripture, or a problem or even a person, and – with God – chew it over and examine it. Look at it intently, from every angle, turning it over in your mind; and ask for God's help to see it in a new and deeper way. Meditation is about seeing anew: taking off the eyes of the world and seeing through a 'God lens'. Taking your head and placing it in your heart.

My friends are my friends because at some point we started talking and spent time together and have been through life together, which has formed a bond and strengthened our connection. They know me and I know them. They love me and I love them. And a fundamental feature of our relationship is communication.

The same is true of our relationship with God. We need to talk with him and spend time with him to get to know him. 'That's all well and good,' you may say, 'but does he actually talk back?' Prayer can sometimes feel like you are speaking into a black cave where nothing comes back. It may feel like this at first, but it does get better. Keep going.

Chapter Six

Self-Worth and Identity

You are not your job, your successes or your failures; nor are you your faults, your emotions, your acts of kindness or your selfish desires. You are all of these things and you are more than them; you are loved. Loved since the beginning of all things, and destined to be loved for eternity. St Francis of Assisi famously prayed, 'God, teach me who you are and teach me who I am.' Knowing and accepting yourself as a flawed yet precious human is a key part of a happy life. Jesus tells us to 'Love your neighbour as you love yourself', so how can you love anybody if you don't love yourself? Loving yourself starts by acknowledging that you are loved and lovable.

God Pod Playlist, Track 6: 'Slip Away' – Perfume Genius

This song feels like the beating drum of our soul reminding us that we are beautiful and divine and to let go of all the noise that gets in the way. To know that we are loved and precious.

May I suggest that we all carry a level of injury within us that causes us to doubt our self-worth and with which we sabotage ourselves? Falling in love with my wife and having her fall in love with me helped me to understand that I was worthy of love. A lot of us struggle with the notion that we are lovable and valuable.

God teaches us as Christians that we are the object of his love, and it's only once we recognise this that we are in a position to love both ourselves and others. People search for love because they want to know they are lovable. Love begets love and is like a flame; think how many flames you can light with one single match. But you must first learn to love yourself, accepting all your weaknesses and flaws, before you can effectively love others. You are only human after all, and we all carry with us our brokenness.

As I mentioned in Chapter Four, at university I went through a difficult patch when I got in with a group of guys who were quite negative. We spent most of our time taking the mick out of each other. I never felt comfortable with that dynamic, and experienced a recurring dream at the time of not being able to open my mouth.

Every time I tried to speak, my teeth caught on each other and my jaw wouldn't move. The only sounds that came out were nonsensical. I was voiceless.

I now recognise this period as a difficult one in my life, as it generated so much fear and anxiety. It was the early days of me being a Christian, and I realised I had to get away from the group. I began to forgive myself for my weakness and allowed myself the grace I often showed others. I came to acknowledge that I felt voiceless because I was in a difficult place in my life, and that even the weak part of me was still worthy of love. This led me to a more holistic view of love, in that true love accepts both the good and the bad in us.

We need to be aware of our weaknesses and tell ourselves it's okay to have flaws as well as strengths, and that we are only trying our best. To be able to generously accept ourselves as we really are is no small feat, as to do so is to let go of our ego and face our true selves. But when we do this and lovingly embrace our whole being, we move to a deeper and more fulfilled place where we are at peace. The more we are able to consciously and serenely acknowledge our own strengths and weaknesses, the better we can live in our own skin. When Jesus says 'Love your neighbour as you love yourself', it is not an excuse to do what we want at all times, but rather about offering ourselves grace. It is from this place of grace that we are more capable of change.

Honesty is so important – not just with ourselves but with others too. We live in an airbrushed age, with social media painting untruths of who we are, and outdated or *polished* profile pictures hiding the real us. Why is it we only celebrate our successes and happy, triumphant moments on Facebook and Instagram? What would happen if we were to post updates when we were feeling down and vulnerable?

When you are down and your morale is low, you need to self-support and also seek support from those that you trust. There is no shame in feeling depressed, and nor is there any point berating or guilt-tripping yourself like Dobby the House Elf in *Harry Potter*, who punishes himself every time he gets something wrong.

I have never felt confident in anything other than the knowledge that I know God and am loved by him. I feel like I can articulate him well to others too. When we hear a truth, a bit of us says, 'I knew that already.' It just makes sense. I felt like this when I came to God.

God wants us to be who we truly are. Even though I ended up studying at Cambridge University through my theological college, I've always felt I wasn't very smart, which is not particularly helpful for my confidence when it comes to teaching. This is because, at school, I was always told I wasn't academic. Add to this my being an identical twin, which brought with it other insecurities . . . Up to the age of nine, Charles and I were in the same class. We were in our own world together, we resonated with and bounced off each other. The teachers couldn't tell us apart and so struggled to deal with us. Eventually, they decided to split us up and put us in separate classes. Charles's output went up and mine went down, so it then looked as if I had been holding him back, and that I was clearly the less intelligent twin and Charles was the academic one – and, by inference, brighter. And those labels stuck. In sports I was a little better – not much, just a little. We then both went to another school together. I didn't have the happiest time there either.

We must be careful about believing in the identities that others give us; incorrect labelling creates low self-esteem that, when combined with mental health issues, can have tragic results. The good news is that when we find the Lord inside us and start believing in him to guide our voice, we can do anything, even flipping a bad reputation we might be carrying for something that happened a long time ago or shedding an unwanted label that's stuck. There is always redemption.

Part of the message of Christ is new creation, fresh life and goodness renewed from death and decay. But I want to be clear here: people who know and have found God can still suffer from mental health issues and depression. Although we have faith, that does not necessarily mean we are wrapped in a bubble of bliss. A number of the greatest saints suffered severe depression, and some scholars believe the great prophet Jeremiah did too. He was known as the 'weeping prophet'.

Those with mental health issues should seek medical help; it's not about white-knuckling and holding on to holy books. God gave us brains and the medical profession, and he meant for us to use them! For while God can heal, it is often through seeking help from the resources he has given to us through his working in humanity that we find the victory.

I think the biggest existential question anyone can ask is 'Who am I?' I believe that my generation is plagued by a lack of identity and not being able to understand who we really are. We look for our identity in all the wrong places, like Instagram and Facebook. And because we're not confident or comfortable with who we are, we present a false image of our life – papering over what we might be going through with doctored images and photos of enviable places we've visited.

While we can know in the deep places of our soul that we are loved, we can still struggle to feel it. My prayer, however, is that we would all know it and experience it. One of the major reasons I am writing this book is that I want to show you that you are all loved and your identity is secure, as it is determined by the one who made us – not what you feel or what the world or others tell you.

I teach a lot about identity in my church. There is a story in the Bible about the Holy Spirit leading Jesus into the desert to be tempted by the Devil. For forty days and nights, Jesus fasts and prays, and the Devil tries to tempt him in three ways. In his first temptation, the Devil slyly says, 'If you are the son of God, turn this stone into bread.' The temptation here is that Jesus would find his identity through what he does. In essence, the Devil is saying, 'You are what you do.'

This idea is prevalent in our society. When we look at others with a judgemental eye, discerning their value based on their level of success, we are on shaky ground. Many a conversation starts like this: 'Hey, what's your name? What do you do?' This line of questioning suggests we are determining a person's value in terms of their economic position. It's as if we are vetting them, in order to know whether the person is worth our time.

This superficial measurement is really destructive for self-esteem. A person's value does not lie in their job. Is a cleaner of less value than a lawyer? No, their inherent value is the same. They were both born naked into this world, and they will both die. Now, their jobs may influence and help people in different ways, which is fine – however, their jobs do not dictate who they are as people, and whether they are a good or a bad individual. Each of us is capable of being proud and selfish, humble and kind. When we allow the job we do to cloud how we see and understand ourselves, it can lead to false notions of self. The key to identity is in knowing that our own value is based on nothing we have done. Our value is a gift given to us by the one who made us, it is not earned, it is inherent; we were made in God's image and that value is priceless. From this place our identity is on a firm foundation of love, knowing we are loved by an unconditional love before we have done anything is a great freedom. When we know our own value, and that we are loved and are at peace, we can then bring value to others.

Certainly, in my life, the people who are kind, compassionate and generous – and who I want to be around – are those who *know* themselves. They do not try to present themselves as something they are not. They know who they are, and they are comfortable with that.

I worked in a homeless shelter for a number of years, and as the priest I was in charge of the spiritual well-being of the guests. There was one guy there (who has sadly now passed on) who was humble and kind and never looked at others judgementally. He felt that God loved him, and he allowed this to fill up his being. He would sleep in train stations, he was not successful financially, and yet he was at peace within himself. His funeral was held at a church for the homeless, and around a hundred people turned up.

As Christians we believe that identity must spring from the knowledge that we are loved by God and infinitely valuable to him, and nothing we do or don't do can affect that. A classic Christian teaching is that there is nothing you can do to make God love you any more than he already does, and there is nothing you can do to make him love you any less.

The second temptation in the Bible is when the Devil takes Jesus to the top of the temple in Jerusalem. Jerusalem was the spiritual heart of the Israelite faith, and the temple was a place of particular connection with God. Matthew 4 records:

> Then the Devil took him to the holy city and had him stand on the highest point of the temple. 'If you are the Son of God,' he said, 'throw yourself down. For it is written: "He will command his angels concerning you, and they will lift you up in their hands, so that you will not strike your foot against a stone."'

So the Devil is saying to Jesus to throw himself down from a high place because the angels will hold him, and that he will, before the eyes of all, glide safely to the ground and not be hurt. This would make everyone plainly see that he was the Messiah and believe it wholeheartedly.

The temptation here is to believe you are what others say you are. Existing on any one of the many social media platforms makes it almost impossible to avoid the gaze of others, and our own gazing back at them and their varied and sometimes enviably presented lives. As recently as fifteen years ago, the only people we had to compete with were our neighbours, colleagues or our friends from school. Now we have to deal with comparing ourselves, unconsciously or otherwise, to millions of people all over the world. These comparisons are unhelpful and sometimes unhealthy, but we can't help but make them.

Almost all of us have online profiles – or personas if you like – and we're each able to carefully curate an idea of ourselves that often may not be a true or accurate representation of what is actually going on inside our heart and mind. It's as if we've become our own publicist or manager, and we want to get the best image of ourselves out there so that we can feel accepted and affirmed by as many people as we can. We may care far too much about what others think about us, and so we take their judgements and perceptions of us as feedback to inform us of who we are. Part of the problem is denial – the failure to know our *real* self, which is prone to anxiety, insecurity and anger on a deeper and more substantial level.

As I mentioned, I'm on Instagram – in fact, that is why I was approached to write this book – and I really enjoy uploading pictures and video clips and sharing my experiences with others and seeing their reactions to my posts. Admittedly, it is a thrill to see so many likes and comments, and I have a relatively large following.

Being a priest, I get a great many direct messages asking me for advice or making prayer requests. I often feel very inadequate when I receive a cry for help from somebody who is really struggling, as there are just too many to be able to answer every single one. I occasionally click on a person's profile to see who is asking for my help. When I follow their link, what I see is a very different story to the one they have just told me. I often see a happy guy or girl, on a beach or in a restaurant; a smiling face in a group of people having fun; or a funny video or a silly meme. But as their messages to me show, this is only one of their faces, and we each have many in our gallery. If you are one of these individuals, I appeal to you to reach out to your local church, visit your doctor or see a therapist who can help you. There is no shame in seeking help.

Social media is not the place to seek an understanding of self, as it's so fickle and the tide of favour can turn very quickly against you. If we allow the words and opinions of others to teach us about ourselves, then we are standing on sand. Just as the sea drains all rivers but never fills up, social media consumes all your time and never blinks as it drinks.

The third temptation happens as the Devil takes Jesus to the top of a high mountain. Matthew records it in his gospel, chapter 4: 'Again, the Devil took him to a very high mountain and showed him all the kingdoms of the world and their splendour. "All this I will give you," he said, "if you will bow down and worship me."'

The temptation is to believe your self-worth is based upon your material possessions, celebrity or status. The world teaches us that we need things – those trainers, that laptop, that jacket – and only once we've accumulated these will we be happy. While it's nice to have new things, shopping for the sake of shopping – rather than buying something because you need it – is just plastering over the void of emptiness that comes from not experiencing the world from the inside out. What I mean is that if we rely on buying things to make us feel good inside, we're living a life dictated by how much we have, rather than finding happiness within ourselves, which doesn't need for anything. Newly purchased gadgets and clothes very swiftly lose their sparkle and are forgotten, and before we know it, we're back in those feeling of discontent, looking for the next hit.

Do your friends make your life easier not harder? Do they love you for being you, despite your weaknesses? Is the relationship a two-way street? Do they build you up rather than making you feel insecure? If you can't answer these questions in the positive, maybe it's time to make some new friends.

You become who you hang out with. If you don't like the people you have chosen to be around, you may be moving to a place where you don't like yourself, and then you're in a destructive spot. Being surrounded by good people makes you feel good, and the fact that they like you reminds you that you are likeable and valued. Though it should go without saying that we are sometimes called to love difficult people, and if you drop everyone that merely annoys you, you will find yourself alone very quickly. Be wise about choosing your friends, as they are one of life's greatest gifts.

Just as we need to be aware of friendships that are damaging or which we have potentially outgrown, it's also important for us to make good choices in our work life. A lot of us get stuck in jobs we don't enjoy, and we become trapped in the nine-to-five grind – mentally only half turning up, and all the while counting down the days till Friday night.

Robert Herrick, the English poet, once wrote: 'Gather ye rose-buds while ye may, / Old Time is still a-flying; / And this same flower that smiles today / Tomorrow will be dying.' We need to remember that life is short, and that it's not good enough to just 'turn up'; we're worth infinitely more than that. It's okay to quit and move on to something/someone else in pursuit of a full life. Remember, you have a choice. And yes, that change might mean taking a pay cut or stepping back to reassess your current path, or not having constant company around you, but it is not worth the damage to your soul and self-esteem to stay in an environment where you feel bullied, oppressed or undervalued.

You need to remind yourself: 'I am worthy of love and value, and this is not teaching me that.' We are called to love all people and recognise the value of everyone. That said, we need to be mindful of those people and places who feed us false or negative narratives – and while we may show them compassion, there is no need to be a slave to their opinion, no rule that you should linger around them. Listen to your own voice, be good to yourself and realise you are loved and valued by God.

Sometimes your own worst enemy is yourself. Your mind bristles with poor opinions of yourself, and feels like it is against you. When I was younger, I often asked myself, 'Brain, aren't you on my side? Why do I always feel like you are fighting me?' As humans, we listen to what our thoughts are constantly telling us, and it's not always positive. But sometimes we need to speak words of compassion, grace and love to ourselves.

Each of us is often our own worst critic, quick to pull ourselves down. As soon as we wake in the morning, our mind quickly goes on the attack with anxious questions or immediate criticisms about how lazy we are, what we failed to do yesterday, and what we are scared of in the coming day. Would you undermine and unsettle your closest friends in this way? So then why do you do it to yourself?

Life is not a sprint race, it's a marathon, and so you need to take regular care of yourself and learn to love who you are. You may not be at the front of the pack with the most expensive trainers on, and you may not have the most impressive house or the best car, but neither do you need to. Run your own race and be kind to yourself; speak softly in your own ear and develop a more forgiving relationship with yourself.

I want you to know that God loves you in all your fragility, even when you doubt yourself. Never forget your worth, and that your very life is a miracle.

Chapter Seven

Positivity

Your outlook affects everything, and if you look at the world judgementally and with cynicism, what you will reap in your heart will be mistrust and bitterness. We need to look outwards from a place of security from within. Call me crazy, but I would rather be proved wrong a couple of times about a person or situation than think everyone is a liar and out to get me. People who lie and cheat will eventually become bitter and angry if they are not that way already, and their punishment is really themselves, so don't waste time on them. Expect good, see the best, go after joy – and when trouble comes, know you will get through it and overcome.

God Pod Playlist, Track 7: 'My Hero' – The Foo Fighters

Purely because it gets me energised and, every time I hear it, I instantly feel encouraged and better about life. The lyrics talk about watching someone you hold as a hero just going about their lives, and knowing they are ordinary and celebrating them for it. You don't need a superpower or a fancy costume to be heroic. I love this song because it tells us that we can all be a hero to somebody, just by being our ordinary selves, and that is a very positive and uplifting thought!

Positivity is the ability to be optimistic and look for silver linings where others only see clouds. A low sense of self-worth will see you blaming yourself and others for things that aren't working in your life, and telling yourself that things will never get better. A positive mindset breeds positive action. Just thinking favourably gives you more energy and bandwidth, making you more open to noticing good things rather than solely focusing on the bad. Are we born negative and pessimistic? No – definitely not. As we grow older, life can get on top of us, and we are constantly challenged by fear and anxiety that can sometimes seem like it's hardwired into our minds. We create mental boundaries where there is really only open horizon.

Life is made up of things that drain us and things that fill us up, and we need a balance in order to be able to flourish. Someone who never exerts themselves will never appreciate the rewards of hard work, while someone who constantly works is missing out on the delight of free time and rest. Imagine a barrel of water, with holes in it. The barrel represents you, while the water contained within is your life energy. The holes in the barrel represent all the things that drain you of your vital spark and make you tired — stressful things, like a difficult work project, a struggling relationship, sickness, family trouble or financial worries. As more and more water drains out through these holes, your precious life energy diminishes and you are left feeling depleted, frustrated and unhappy. In order to block the negative moods that can so easily descend on us, we need fillers — activities that increase our energy and feed our soul, like a tap topping up our barrel. For me, my go-to fillers are sport, music, movies, exercise, hanging out with friends and laughter.

It may come as no surprise to you that personal prayer, stillness and times of worship are also fillers for me. There's a piece of scripture that says 'God gives us a peace that surpasses all understanding', and this is true in my experience; cultivating a relationship with God can generate a peace that rises up in you and is not determined by your environment. So, while all around you may be chaotic, you have a sense of peace within you.

When Jenny went into labour with our first child, Rose, the baby was breaching — meaning she was facing the wrong way round in the birth canal. Doctors and nurses ran around as an alarm went off, signalling an emergency. I was told to get into scrubs, and sign a disclaimer so they could carry out an emergency C-section. We were rushed through into an operating room full of people, with lights flashing and sounds beeping all round us. And yet through all this, Jenny and I had this overwhelming sense of peace.

I remember the anaesthetist saying, 'You two have an odd calmness about you.' I suppose the peace we felt emanated from our trust in God and his love for us.

But I digress! If you have too many holes and not enough fillers, you will operate at a constantly low ebb that may potentially lead to burnout and mental breakdown, or at the very least transform you over time into a lesser version of yourself. Try to find a balance between what must be done and doing what makes you happy. If I have my fillers in place, I then have a structure that supports me and helps me to have the energy and ability to thrive; my work is better, my overall capacity for life increases and I am a happier person.

If you're feeling down, it's good to be honest with yourself, with others you trust and, if you're a religious person, with your God. Sometimes well-meaning people might say, 'Have faith, you'll get through it,' but that's no balm when you're struggling and it's really tough. When someone glibly tells you to 'be positive' it can feel more like a rebuke, as if what they're really saying is 'Get over it and get on with it!'

When I lived in Tanzania, one of the African greetings was '*Habari gani?*' – a kind of 'How's your day going?' – to which the response was always 'N*ʒuri ʒana*', which means 'I'm fine, thanks'. I think in the three years I was there, I never had anyone say, 'I'm not great actually.' It's as if being honest about how we are feeling is forbidden. Of course it's not just in Tanzania this happens, it's a pretty universal thing; and it's certainly very common in West London, where my church is based.

My wife calls me the eternal optimist. I like to joke that it has something to do with my B+ blood type! But I've been lucky enough to have always seen things as half-full rather than half-empty. Whereas Jenny can veer more towards melancholy, and sometimes I need to pep her up with a little encouragement.

Those of you who have experienced being parents probably will remember (or are currently experiencing) getting up in the middle of the night when your kids were babies. No matter how much we love our children, the sleep deprivation in the first few years can be soul-destroying. When our little girl Saoirse cried out for Jenny to breastfeed her in the middle of the night, she would on some occasions understandably groan and say, 'Tell me something positive, Chris.' To which I'd reply: 'Our children are so beautiful and wonderful to be around, and you're a fantastic mother. I appreciate you and everything you do for our children, and they appreciate you too, even though they're not able to tell you yet.' It would remind Jenny that she wanted to do it rather than feeling compelled to. Anything to make her feel that getting up at 3 a.m. was a good thing!

Being optimistic is a way of consciously reframing things; we have a choice as to whether we see situations through a positive frame or a negative one. That said, sometimes there is nothing more exhausting than being around a *relentless* optimist – because, after a time, it can start to feel forced, inauthentic, and honestly like they're a bit delusional! I believe that a true optimist (which I hope I am) wears a genuine smile; and while *they* may be anchored in positivity, they possess the empathy to acknowledge what other people might be going through.

Optimism is infectious and magnetic, but how can we say 'Be happy' in an un-infuriating way? Telling someone to cheer up can sound patronising or even rude if the tone seems insincere or impatient. You can't make someone happy; they have to get there of their own accord. But you can listen to them and try to understand what it is that is blocking them from feeling joy.

If we are feeling negative, one technique to compel ourselves to feel better is to make ourselves smile. If that sounds a bit left-field or fake, then let me explain. Science has proven that the action of smiling can help bolster the immune system, lighten your mood and even extend the length of your life. A happy life is often a long life. When we smile, it sends a message to the brain to relax and produce serotonin, the chemical responsible for lowering stress. Smiling also makes the brain produce dopamine, the chemical that makes us happy. So, if you're feeling blue or depressed, you have the power to lighten the feeling just by smiling, even if you don't mean it. And very quickly, you will be experiencing genuine feelings of contentment. When you smile, the muscles in your mouth move, sending a signal to your brain that you are happy. The brain can be easily – though not always – fooled by this and doesn't always bother to check whether it is authentic joy that is causing the smile.

How can we learn to look at things in a more optimistic light? There are a few Christian writers who talk about being able to step back from your thoughts and the brain's automatic processing (a kind of sleepwalking while awake) to consider your mood from a removed distance, in order to have more control over yourself. One in particular was an amazing guy in the sixteenth century called Ignatius of Loyola, the founder of the Jesuits. At first, he was a young womaniser with little time for God, who just wanted to be a soldier and get all the glory. But in a battle in 1521, his legs were severely injured and he became bedbound. In the house in which he convalesced, there were only two books available for him to read: *The Life of Christ* and *The Lives of the Saints*. Reading these books again and again, over a two-year period, he experienced a religious awakening and observed that it was his drive towards God which sustained him on a deeper level – and which gave him long-term hope rather than flash-in-the-pan desires of military glory.

Upon his recovery, instead of resuming his pursuit of women and fame, he moved towards a holy life. His *Spiritual Exercises* are a group of writings in which he focuses on prayer and meditation. Ignatius was very much a person who said, 'Use your imagination in combination with God and the Holy Spirit to help your prayer life.' He asks us to imagine being in a scene and inviting God into that scene, then seeing where he leads you; opening up your daydreams to God and allowing him to fill them.

Ignatius talked about mapping the mind using two governing principles: 'consolation' and 'desolation'. He believed that someone with a consolation mindset turns towards love, hope, goodness, peace and gentleness; while someone whose mind is drawn to desolation will likely turn inwards in a selfish way that is fuelled by pride, fear, lust, envy or greed – certainly they will not feel in flow with God. Ignatius advised that when we feel distanced from God and spiritually shut down, we should resume our habits of consolation – be it reading the Bible, engaging in prayer, going to church, volunteering, or speaking with a loved one – until we feel close to him again. In a sense, this is a Christian version of fixing a smile to your face to kid your brain, only on a spiritual level.

On any given day you can oscillate wildly between moments of consolation and desolation. The more you learn to listen to your inner self, observing yourself neutrally by listening for the negative thoughts passing through your mind and acknowledging that they are ephemeral and not representative of the real you, the easier it is to recognise when your feelings are being driven by such negative thoughts towards a place of desolation. By being aware of the desolation mindset, you can reset yourself and move towards the positive. It's basically a version of cognitive behavioural therapy (CBT) which helps us to recognise and replace the lies we tell ourselves – *I'm not capable, I'm not good enough, I'm disgusting* – with more positive truths – *you deserve this, you're a good person, you can do it, you are strong.*

By being more conscious of the damaging negative messages we direct at ourselves, we can be at the ready to replace them with positive ones, gently guiding our emotional state and avoiding being washed along by negative currents of thought. I think as I've grown older, I've developed more of an understanding of the various pendulum swings of my heart – from sadness to joy and back again – and, by being mindful of them when they happen, I have more control over them than I used to.

Putting positive practices in place to help my perception and outlook is both important and helpful. Kind self-talk, for example, might sound like: 'I am loved and the people around me are also loved (even the annoying ones)'; 'I am of great value to God'; 'I am forgiven'; 'Though I may be weak at times, God is strong and he loves me'; Nothing can snatch me from his hand, I am not alone'. It's as if I've now become familiar with the instances of negative self-talk that come up again and again, and now I can name them for the false narratives they truly are, I find myself empowered to dismiss them. In *The Art of War*, Sun Tzu says, 'If you know the enemy and know yourself, you need not fear the result of a hundred battles.' He believed that if you know yourself and your enemy – which in our context here is our negative thoughts and ensuing moods – you will be victorious. If you understand yourself and your behaviours and take time to understand where your thoughts and ensuing moods originate from – both the happy and unhelpful ones – you will eventually be better at disposing of the negative ones. If you only know a bit of yourself and shy away from understanding the nature and origins of your darker moods, then you will be less successful in dealing with them.

*

The Bible says, 'With the Lord, a day is like a thousand years, and a thousand years are like a day.' This has been interpreted in various ways. One reading is that God's view of time is different than ours because he is eternal, and while our lives are short in comparison – and so for us, time is precious and can be wasted – for him time does not exist in the same way. My personal take on it is that whatever happened yesterday is now in the past and cannot be changed, but you can choose to live this new day afresh, positively and hopefully, and shine your light and compassion on others: 'This is the day the Lord has made; let us rejoice and be glad in it.'

This thought helped me turn over a new leaf at university when I was coming out of that dark period when I felt lost and stifled. The fact that I could say 'Today has so much potential and space to do positive things' helped me enormously. God's mercies are replenished every morning and our days are blank pieces of paper waiting to be written on with positive acts, if only we can just realise it. We have the chance to change for the better every day and at any point of any day.

Positivity is a close cousin of gratitude. It's important to cultivate gratitude constantly, for the more grateful you are, the more life opens up to you and the more positive you become. Gratitude for what you have rather than longing for what you don't have is instrumental to your happiness. And working towards a happy mind can lead to better sleep, greater satisfaction and improved physical health, with less fatigue and more energy – energy that can help you build a positive and self-renewing momentum so that the next day, and all the days after, can feel even more full of possibility and opportunities for positive acts.

Psalm 100:4 says that we should 'Enter His gates with thanksgiving.' Giving thanks brings us into God's presence. There's something about having a thankful heart that positions us in the right frame of mind to make the best of things. As soon as I wake up, I intentionally start the day with a thankful positive breath before my thoughts drift elsewhere and start trying to make me anxious. I think of all the wonderful things I have to be grateful for, and this sets me up for a positive day.

In Tanzania I lived by myself in a compound, and on the wall of my room I pinned about a hundred of my favourite pieces of scripture. I would go to this wall as soon as I got up every morning, close my eyes and then let my finger fall randomly on one of the scriptures, and I'd read it and take that scripture as my positive springboard for the day ahead. By choosing to dictate the start of my day, I was consciously avoiding being a passenger carried along on an unconscious current of my thoughts.

For you, maybe this could take the form of a vision board – a therapeutic collage – put up in a prominent place and approached with feelings of gratitude. This could involve pictures, words, or anything else that is meaningful to help bring positive energy into your life. Or maybe you could create a list of positive and empowering mantras about yourself which you repeat over and over. What you repeatedly tell the mind, it will soon accept.

Our brains work a bit like an internet search engine and those targeted online ads – you get out what you put in. Type something into your internet search bar and you get lists of things on whatever subject you're searching for. As we continue to use the internet and search around, an algorithm watches for patterns in our online behaviour and gradually builds a picture of what it thinks we're interested in seeing, and then it shows us more of the same sort of stuff through these targeted ads. Similarly, if I look out onto the world through fearful and worried eyes, everything I see will be framed by my fear and worry. But if we start searching around us for good things, our brain's algorithm and patterns of thought will eventually learn that we're no longer as interested in focusing on the bad stuff that brings us down, and we will more readily be able to see more and more of the things that bring us joy.

I want to encourage you to look at the world and ask: 'Where can I find goodness? Where is there hope? Where can I find positivity?' Once you start using more positive search terms, the results shift dramatically, and you start seeing the world through a more uplifting lens that will filter out negativity.

As you look at the world and search for answers and meaning, try your best to actively look through an optimistic lens as you go through each day. It may feel strange or even jarring at first, but over time your patterns of thought will shift to be more in step with your active optimism, and you will find that it slowly becomes easier to see the good in everything around you.

The different mindsets we adopt directly steer the mood we'll experience on any given day. Making a smoothie for yourself and taking exercise are both statements of self-love. Although exercise is tiring, the pay-off is a hit of dopamine (the reward chemical in the brain) and a corresponding feeling of happiness and well-being. Forty minutes' running is so much more self-nourishing than zoning out and watching Netflix for hours at a time.

The spark of genius that separates man from animals is the gift of choice, allowing us to be masters of our own destiny through the decisions we make. In Deuteronomy, the Bible says, 'I have set before you life and death, blessing and cursing. So choose life so that you and your descendants may live.' For those of you reading this who suffer from poor mental health, I fully understand that it's not always easy for you to dictate your mood in the morning. Self-love and kindness are vital steps on your journey back to a healthier place, as is reaching out to get the help you need. These are positive measures.

Thankfulness and generosity are also close cousins. Being generous doesn't just mean with your finances; it is also about your time and your services. Thankful people are more generous, and generous people are usually more thankful. And the more grateful you are, the more you notice the myriad reasons to be optimistic. Looking on the bright side is a habit you can form without too much effort, but you need to practise constant self-maintenance in order to achieve it.

*

Even amidst the great highs in our lives we can carry a sense of desolation – in the midst of life, we are in death – just as in the great lows we can find elements of consolation. As a Christian, I believe that in heaven there will be no more tears, no more pain, and that we will live in a perpetual understanding of God's blessing and presence around us. But in this life, we are frequently exposed to sorrow and pain, and I think that there is something very powerful in being able to navigate those moments with hope, saying, 'This will pass.' External events will try to dictate how you should act and feel, but ultimately you can decide how to shape your attitude – be it one of resignation and surrender or hope and positivity. When all is said and done, you are the captain of your soul. I believe that the only thing that keeps us separate from God is our thought that we are separate from God.

It is essential to acknowledge pain – both physical and emotional – but try not to wallow in it, or allow it to be bigger than you. Equally, don't attempt to lock it away or repress it, as it will fester, infecting your psyche. Remember that you are not defined by your pain, and nor should you allow yourself to be ruled by it. Being able to name our emotions without becoming restrained by them is a necessary step towards optimism and happiness; a way of navigating to a place outside of the impulsive emotional maelstrom, and looking back on it as a distanced observer in order to be more objective. Choosing to be positive is about going to a deeper place which speaks truth, life and love to you.

*

With so many technological advances these days, we can sometimes become overly cerebral and too much in our own heads. We need to listen to our bodies and not just our minds, and activities like dancing, Pilates and sport in general are great for helping us to reconnect with our breathing and improve our well-being. Rushing is the curse of our age, especially in cities and towns, and sitting in stillness in the morning is something that really helps me to slow down. And let's not forget the Zs! Getting enough sleep is vital to maintaining a happy self. Listen to your body when it's tired in the evening, and respect it sufficiently to go to sleep when it asks you to; most of us need around seven or eight hours of uninterrupted sleep to flourish mentally and physically. Similarly, choosing to eat healthy food – mindfully and appreciatively – will also make you feel better. When eating, remember that the food you're consuming once grew from a seed or walked upon the earth as a living, breathing creature. Don't wolf it down; savour it and be thankful for the nourishment it is giving you.

Practising gratitude every day shifts your energy rapidly and is cited by many as a major building block of contentment. So, my friends, cultivate a grateful soul, look for things to make you smile, and be aware of what is going through your mind and how much positive input there is.

Chapter Eight

Humble Confidence

Humility is not so much a case of thinking less of yourself, but rather thinking of yourself less. I always have to say that twice to let it sink in! Humility is the good soil in which every good character trait is grown. We should be able to laugh at ourselves and have others laugh at us without becoming defensive; we should know our place and who we are without anyone else needing to tell us; and if and when it is required we should be ready and willing to step up and explore new things when others won't. Humility doesn't seek the limelight and need praise, but it doesn't shrink back from opportunity or responsibility either. In nature, the peacock is beautiful and seeks attention, but the snow leopard is rare, beautiful and powerful – and I would rather see the snow leopard. Humble confidence is equally rare, beautiful and powerful.

God Pod Playlist, Track 8: 'Can I Kick It?' – A Tribe Called Quest

This song has a humble strength; its relaxed yet powerful hook reminds me that true strength doesn't exert itself but rests confidently in its own truth – that it can and will overcome.

I f we don't know who we truly are, we will look for meaning in needless things. The motto 'know thyself' first appeared inscribed on the forecourt of the Temple of Apollo at Delphi. Among the many ancient Greek philosophers that adopted this maxim and interrogated it, Socrates believed that to really understand yourself, you need to be fully aware of your strengths and weaknesses as well as the way you react to things – and the only route to achieving this self-knowledge is by regular introspection and constant questioning.

When we come across people who understand themselves better than the rest of us do, it's as if they are more at home in their skin, because they know their value and trust themselves. They radiate a glow of self-confidence that manages never to come across as arrogance, and we often feel drawn to them and want to be around them. True peace can only be found by looking inward. It doesn't depend on Instagram likes, and nor does it need designer clothes or a swanky car to flourish.

So, what is it about a self-possessed person that is so magnetic? Perhaps because their company makes us feel valued or inspires us, and we feel we can learn from them. Such a person is open to feedback and acknowledges it with grace, even if they don't fully agree with it. Humble confidence is about letting your actions and their results speak for themselves, instead of advertising every good thing you do for everyone to know about. When you have humble confidence, you don't actively seek the spotlight but are comfortable when you find yourself in it, as long as it serves a positive purpose. You are not the loudest voice in the room, and yet your presence is so much stronger than those who feel the need to be heard all the time. A person with humble confidence feels sufficiently comfortable in their own skin to let others do the talking, but if they feel something is wrong they can also stand up and be counted in the moments when it truly matters. The very word 'humble' has its linguistic roots in the ancient Greek word *humus*, meaning 'earth'. While a person with humble confidence can rise to the occasion and shine, they are always safely anchored, grounded and down to earth.

I remember meeting a businessman in London whose job involved buying ailing companies and reviving them. In his line of work, it was as if he had the Midas touch. I saw him sitting in his car before a talk he was to give; he'd arrived ahead of time and so was ready to begin his presentation on the dot. He had a grace about him and, despite his great success and billionaire wealth, he was incredibly modest. He was one of those people where you just felt like you could trust him. He told us that, when recruiting at a high level, the most important thing he looked for in a person was character – how would they affect others around them?

Character is formed through experience, which through self-introspection can be transformed into wisdom. To develop wisdom, we need to be able to learn from our mistakes, taking responsibility for our actions and the impact they have on others. Through this, we become more empathetic. The more resilient we are around our failures, seeing them as pathways to success and greater understanding, the more likely we are to succeed, and through these successes we develop self-esteem. Humble confidence is grounded in having failed and learned from that failure; having been through adversity and grown from the experience.

Take Roger Federer – possibly the best tennis player the world has ever seen. He has grace, passion and authenticity in spades, and is quietly confident about his craft. He's also as dignified in losing as he is in moments of victory. People with humble confidence are always grateful for what they have rather than what they don't have. They don't feel the need to criticise and judge others in order to feel safe or good about themselves. Being around someone like that – who seeks to live a life which is loving and giving – feels like nutrition for your soul.

Humble confidence brings peace to those who have it, and also to all those who are around it. If we could all cultivate a deeper sense of who we are, we'd be happier people – keener to listen to and understand others, less reactionary, less aggressive. Humble confidence is about knowing your flaws, being at peace with them, and having conviction in what you say, do and believe in. In other words, walking your talk – and being authentic, honest and real in everything you do.

St Francis of Assisi said, 'O Divine Master, grant that I may not so much seek . . . to be understood as to understand . . .' Humble confidence allows you to listen and be present in your conversations with others, because you don't feel the need to constantly fight to be heard. The more at peace we are with ourselves, the less of a need there is to sell our virtues and successes to others, and the more generous we can be with our listening. It's lovely when you know someone is genuinely interested in what you have to say, compared with those one-way conversations where the other person hardly seems to be listening when you speak.

Have you ever noticed someone's face start to glaze over when the conversation drifts away from them? We probably all do it sometimes, if we're really being honest with ourselves – listen with half an ear to what someone else is saying, but we're really just waiting for an opening to introduce our story or add our opinion to the conversation. We're listening to them speak, but all the while we're waiting for our turn to speak.

That doesn't sound like great listening to me. In fact, we might call that 'hearing' rather than listening. Truly listening is a generous act, and seeks to understand the other person over and above the need to be understood ourselves.

Sometimes when I'm around a person I feel inferior to – especially if I'm feeling a bit low in myself – I find myself trying to impress them with my successes, telling them about my achievements and metaphorically putting all my medals and awards out on display in an attempt to get their approval. Although I'm talking myself up in the moment, afterwards I'm always left feeling empty and diminished by the conversation, or lack of it. While I'm trying hard to build myself up for this person and mask my insecurities, it usually becomes a very one-sided conversation and I've ended up doing all the talking.

The opposite of this is when I feel my inner barrel is full of confidence and peace, and I'm easily able to navigate conversations or interactions with new people or people of authority and influence. Humble confidence is about being comfortable in your own skin, and not relying on your successes or failures to determine the way you interact with others. Once you find that natural rhythm in yourself, simply existing becomes so much more fluid.

A friend of mine is a successful journalist and author who has spent the last fifteen years travelling the world. He's been lucky enough to dive with sperm whales, track Kodiak bears, and experience some other truly extraordinary adventures. When his stories appear in newspapers as impressive double spreads, his father-in-law often says, 'You hide your light under a bushel' – meaning he thinks my friend is too modest about his achievements. Nowadays, especially in careers like journalism, self-promotion is very common and accepted as just another part of the job. Some news outlets measure the 'success' of an article by looking at the amount of views it generates – which doesn't necessarily correlate with the quality of the writing – and they rely on 'clickbait' headlines to pique our curiosity and encourage us to look. But while my friend sometimes shares his articles online in order to help them reach as many people as possible, he tries not to measure his self-worth by seeing his name in a newspaper byline or how many likes he gets.

Now, let me be the first to acknowledge that being a Church of England vicar and an Instagram influencer is a fairly unusual combination. I've been interviewed many times by the press, in newspapers and on TV, and one question I'm consistently asked is whether I feel a sense of conflict between trying to gain followers and being a priest, which is a role that seems to contradict the idea of self-promotion. I think this is a fair question, and I have grappled with it on and off over the years. For me, the key to answering this comes in asking myself why I do what I do online. Is it simply to grow a personal platform, for the purpose of inflating my ego and self-esteem? On reflection, I don't think so. It's that I feel called to speak light and life into what can often feel like a dark and superficial place.

One morning in my personal prayer time, I was reading Acts 17 when this particular verse jumped off the page: 'All the Athenians and the foreigners who lived there spent their time doing nothing but talking about and listening to the latest ideas.' The next verses go on to say that St Paul stood up and spoke to them about the unknown God. This resonated with me, because I feel like social media platforms are places where everyone gathers to talk and listen and share the latest ideas, but they often *do* nothing and feel directionless. Like Paul, I had the feeling that God was calling me to stand up in and among these people, and point them towards God.

The difference between humble confidence and self-praise on these platforms lies in your reason for using them. Ask yourself honestly: are you posting to receive validation and to feel loved and better about yourself? Do you do it to generate followers, or to keep your brand or business afloat by making sure the greatest audience knows all about it? 'Know thyself' also means to know your motivations. Be brutally honest with yourself in order to understand where yours are coming from. Social media feeds have become linked with self-promotion and brand-building, but using them purely to share things that might make others happy or to keep in touch with friends is the most humble way of all.

True humble confidence is about backing yourself and striving to achieve your full potential, not feeling the need to shout about yourself at the expense of listening to the larger conversation. It also requires a willingness to call yourself out when you realise you've got something wrong.

Sometimes we view our social interactions in terms of economics: 'What is the point of this exchange, what will I get out of it?' But it may be more useful to reframe this attitude to one of 'What can I discover about this person, what is fascinating about them, what are their stories?' Two of my best friends are Andy and Sho. Like me, they also occasionally appear as guests on the Jolly

YouTube channel. This channel along with the KoreanEnglishman channel, run by my brother in-law Ollie and friend Josh, is where I first spoke to a younger generation about faith. Appearing on these channels was the catalyst that threw me into the online world. If you want a laugh, I recommend watching some of their videos online! I find the way Andy and Sho communicate with other people totally amazing; they have such a curious mindset and have the gift of making people feel at ease and that they are really being listened to. If only their curiosity in others could be bottled and sold! They can sit in a taxi and, by the end of the ride, the cabbie doesn't want to charge them. They'll strike up a conversation with complete strangers and end up being invited to stay with them, and they actually follow through and go to visit them.

Their secret? They help others feel valued. I'm always in awe watching them at events like weddings, because unlike most of us – who, if we're honest, would prefer to spend our time talking with our friends – they are always eager to meet new people and hear their stories. They have a way of seeing a wealth in others, which they manage to effortlessly coax out of them by being magnificent listeners.

When people feel listened to, it has a powerful and warm effect on them. I often say, 'To love well is to listen well.' Ask yourself, are you listening to someone to understand them, or are you waiting to be heard – waiting for an opportunity to show your medals and trophies?

Fullness of life is about finding wholeness in yourself, humanity, the earth and God, and appreciating the miracle which is you – and the person to your left and to your right. The most interesting and engaging people I have met are those who are successful in what they do but are humble with it. Despite their high-ranking positions, they possess not only a sense of authority and a gravitas but also an air of humility.

Leaders like Nelson Mandela and Gandhi are like firmly anchored, deep-rooted trees, and their hidden depths make them compelling and magnetic. Less is always more. The fruit of their lives is there for all to see, but they make no point of directing you towards it. It's in the shade of such trees that I like to sit.

One of the interesting things about Jesus is that he didn't live up to his potential. He was the son of God, imbued with all the power of his father; he led twelve men, then died alone on a cross. He could have commanded the seas and the skies and the mountains to fall on anyone. He could have been the emperor of the universe if he wanted to. But instead, he washed his disciples' feet, he died for them, and he died for us. He didn't achieve his potential, but he did satisfy his calling.

Jesus's teaching on love is, I think, the most powerful teaching the world has ever recieved: 'A new commandment I give you: love one another. As I have loved you, so you must love one another' (John 13:34). He is the purest example of humble confidence I can think of.

So, how do we follow the road of humble confidence? We go about our business with quiet grace. We are confident in our abilities, but don't need to shout about ourselves and our successes in order to be noticed. We constantly try to know ourselves, through introspection and by being aware of our strengths, weaknesses, fears and true motivations. We listen to others to understand them, not so that we can satiate our egos by simply waiting for our turn to speak. And finally, we are authentic, grounded, and true to our inner selves.

Chapter Nine

Leadership

Being a leader can be lonely – making decisions, taking action, being the one who has to make the call. Leadership is not about always knowing the course ahead, but it is about having the courage to choose a destination and walk there, and to bring others along with you. We often talk about the Lord as a shepherd, who leads us to green pastures and still waters. Just as the sheep trust in their shepherd and allow themselves to be guided by him, trusting in his judgement, so we let ourselves be guided by God. How can you be a better shepherd, a better leader, to those in your life?

God Pod Playlist, Track 9: 'Turn the Page' – The Streets

To be a leader is to sometimes be alone, but this isolation is for the benefit of the whole – to love them, to give courage to them and bear with them. This song speaks to me of this service and sacrifice. (And, random fact: I was actually in the music video for their song 'Weak Become Heroes' and shook Mike Skinner's hand . . . Pretty cool, eh?!)

We remember Jesus as the Good Shepherd. A shepherd is a strong and hardy type who leads their sheep through storms, snow and rainfall, and puts themselves between their flock and danger when fending off predators. A shepherd would never abandon their sheep, and will lead them to places of nourishment and refreshment where they can find food and rest.

Psalm 23 says, 'The Lord is my shepherd . . . He makes me lie down in green pastures, he leads me beside still waters.' Christians know that Jesus is our shepherd, that he is strong, and with us and courageous, and that he will never leave us. More broadly, a shepherd guides and protects a community. Leading with kindness and compassion, as Jesus did, keeps your flock together; protecting and supporting a community helps it to flourish and grow. In this chapter we'll look at how we can be better shepherds – better leaders – to those in our lives.

When I was at theological college, I was advised not to become friends with my parishioners, as it's assumed you can't adequately pastor someone from a position of friendship and it needs a level of distance. However, I disagree with that, as it feeds into the idea that a priest should be untouchable or somehow out of reach. This common problem is referred to as clericalism. I've found that quite the opposite has happened, quite organically, as many of my friends whom I already loved and cared for also happen to be members of our church. This intimate love and respect make both our community and our church a lot stronger. In John 15, Jesus says to his disciples, 'I no longer call you servants, because a servant does not know his master's business. Instead, I have called you friends, for everything that I learned from my Father I have made known to you.'

Pop into any bookstore and you'll see that there are myriad books on leadership and the different styles people can adopt to lead others, although mainly with business, profit and productivity at the forefront of the authors' minds. Arguably, the single-minded pursuit of economic growth has left the world in bad shape. Leaders need to realise that there is more to life than profit. And, as leaders, we need to be captains of our own ships before we try to lead others; that is to say, we need to identify and examine our own drives and desires, and understand how they affect us. This is what I'd call leading from the inside out.

When I arrived at my church in West London for the first time, I inherited a team that was used to the way things had always been done there and who worked very differently to me. To be fair to them, they had been in survival mode, trying to keep the lights on and ensure that some sort of worship continued in the church. But they weren't happy or thriving, just surviving. It had been tough for them, and they were tired; and so, at the beginning, they looked upon me and all my changes with some degree of fear.

The hardest thing to change in any environment is the culture. It can take years, but then when the culture does shift there is sudden progress. There was very little drive or hope when I first arrived at St Saviour's. Instead of being a place of faith-filled and buoyant ambition, the atmosphere was defeatist and pessimistic. So I tried to foster courage and faith, as well as a bit of risk-taking.

I often say that indecision is worse than making the wrong decision. It's easy to run from potential conflict and cling to the status quo. But it's only once we start making decisions – and judge ourselves not by success or failure, but by our ability to take action and create momentum – that we make progress. At the beginning of my service I made some mistakes, and I could have dealt with some things differently, but making decisions moved us forward and set in people's minds that we were heading somewhere new.

On my first Sunday at the church, I preached from a different location to where the past preachers had spoken from, and relocated the lectern to the centre of the sanctuary. I wanted to show the congregation that things were going to change, that I was going to do things differently, that this wasn't just another Sunday.

I then motioned to discuss moving from pews to chairs. The church had already thought about this – the pews were very heavy and not very comfortable – but funds were tight. There was some opposition at first, but a year later everyone saw the benefits; and even my harshest critic admitted that the chairs have actually been really good for the church community.

I was really proud when no one left the church after my arrival, which can sometimes happen when a new preacher takes over. Gradually people began to trust me more and I saw the fruits of my labours as our community started to grow. Over time, we invited new people to join in with the leadership of the church, and as a result we are now so much stonger and established. It is a true joy to lead them.

A good leadership lesson is to look for where life is, and invest in it to see yet more life spring forth. Imagine you are a farmer trying to discover which crop is best-suited to your soil. You sow it with different seeds to see what takes root. That which grows is the thing to invest in, for it has the best chance of surviving. When Steve Jobs returned to run Apple in the mid-1990s he jettisoned many ongoing projects, choosing to streamline development and focus on the release of the colourful iMac. He saw where the life was and invested in it.

Let me give you another example . . . My church started a Mums and Tots group for families in our area, which evolved from conversations with a few mothers who were struggling. I'd suggested we start something they could come to where their kids could be safe and have fun, and in turn we could invest time in the children and their parents. This quickly grew in popularity, and many parents decided to baptise their kids as a result. We then tried another regular event – a speaker's evening – but that turned out to be very poorly attended. So we took notice of what worked and what didn't, and decided to invest our time and effort into where the life was – where the community showed it needed us. We abandoned the speaker's evening and put even more energy into the Mums and Tots group.

At the end of each year, I ask myself two questions: What was the most *exciting* thing/situation/person I experienced? And what was the most *successful* thing I did? Once I've examined the answers and found the life in each, I look to invest in it and expand from there. For example, we gave our Mums and Tots group a special budget and looked into what resources we could provide so it could better serve the community. We also re-examined and identified its purpose – to help struggling parents – and kept that at its centre to ensure that we did not lose sight of the vital reasons for which it had been started. We didn't just want to deliver a professional service to the parents and children in our church community; we were also looking for ways in which we could better help those parents and give greater support to local families. If they then felt like coming to a church service, then great – but it wasn't just about increasing our numbers.

When I think of strong leadership, the Queen of England comes to mind. She is calm, consistent, measured and full of integrity, and for this reason people listen to her and believe her. Likewise, I admire Pope Francis for the authenticity his actions possess. An ex-bouncer and former literature teacher, he lived and worked as a priest in the slums of Buenos Aires and is passionate about ending inequality – and he routinely pressures governments to close the wealth gap between the rich and poor. He drives a thirty-year-old beat-up Renault, refuses to sleep in the Papal Palace, is unafraid to speak out against corruption and the Italian Mafia, and regularly sneaks out of the Vatican at night to visit the homeless of Rome and give them money – *and* he has nearly twenty million followers on Twitter!

I ascribe my own success on Instagram to people wanting to see an authentic person of faith. There's not much sophistication to my sixty-second sermons, but they're simple and true to who I am. At the moment, I think there's a vacuum of honesty in a great many leaders. In its place, we see selfish ambition, scaremongering and a lack of accountability as dominant forces. We're not seeing enough genuine care, love or authenticity in those we follow.

Personally, I look to the anointed leaders – the saints, like St Francis of Assisi – to inspire me. St Francis chose not to criticise the power-hungry, fat-cat clergy of the time, but to show a better way by living his life as a good example; he lived simply and loved the poor. My style of leadership is an open and loving one, and I am honest with my church members – although there have been tricky times where I haven't felt 100 per cent. One time, as I started to preach for the Sunday service, I realised I felt wounded and a bit all over the place. My mind was elsewhere, worrying about things I couldn't change, and I couldn't concentrate on what I was saying.

I was preaching, but my inner monologue was off-kilter and I actually had to stop mid-sermon. I apologised, and everyone was very kind and waited while I gathered myself. After a breath and a swift silent prayer, I found my resolve and continued. I didn't want to fake it and pretend to them that I was okay when inside I was suffering. I'm glad I look that moment to get my head straight, and I am grateful that my parishioners were supportive of that.

Being honest with your team builds trust, because when they know you are as human as they are and that you're happy to reveal your weaknesses – something which I believe is actually a great strength – they too will trust you with their authentic selves. It is well documented that both Julius Caesar and Alexander the Great rolled up their sleeves, got their hands dirty and led from the front. Alexander would be the first man in his army to engage with the enemy, astride his magnificent black horse Bucephalus. When Caesar was soldiering in Gaul, he often slept under the night sky alongside his men, beneath his shield and wearing a simple tunic.

In Tanzania, I learned a great deal about leadership – and about life in general. My time there taught me that we can find our way around most problems, and that we are much more resourceful than we think we are. A particular story sticks firmly in my memory where this is concerned.

One morning, some people came to me as a decision-maker to help them out of a hole . . . quite literally, as it happened. A cow – *their* cow – had fallen into a newly laid deep-drop toilet. Fortunately, it was brand new so there was no slurry in it, which would have made it a little more fragrant! When we got there, we attached one rope around the body of the cow and then to our Land Rover; and then we tied another rope around the cow to be held by three men on the opposite side of the hole, so they could pull the cow away from the side of the pit as the Land Rover pulled the animal up. One thing I am quite good at is being able to assign jobs to others which bring out their natural skills. My brother Charles was visiting at the time, so I selected him as the one to drive the Land Rover. He's in the army, so he's learned how to be cool and collected in a crisis. It felt a bit like a military operation!

A good leader knows when to listen, when to empathise and when to encourage and inspire. Jesus wasn't choking on his own sense of importance; he was a great listener. You know, most of the miracles that Jesus performed happened when people interrupted him while he was on a journey to somewhere else. He was okay with human interruption, and he used these moments to listen and to heal people. When people are too busy for others all the time, there's a problem. I've worked with leaders who have no time for you and hide behind their 'packed schedules'; and I've worked with those who, despite being time-poor, try to create space in order to help you. A good shepherd will lead the members of his flock in many different ways: sometimes it's from the front; or if they know where they are going, he will lead from the back to support them; or sometimes he will be in amongst them. A shepherd is not this squeaky clean individual who sits and gazes at the setting sun, but rather a rugged and sweat-sodden leader with a crook who protects and defends his flock.

My own leadership style is to share control but keep my personal accountability high, and it's important to me to put faith in people and empower them to do a good job using their own initiative. In some ways, being a priest is a bit like running your own business, but instead of employees you have volunteers – and given that people are often time-poor and exhausted from their busy lives, getting them involved in church life can be a challenge. So how can I gain commitment from these people so that our work gains traction? I believe I can achieve this is by creating a vision they feel they want to invest in, via social transformation projects such as helping the homeless, and by cultivating an atmosphere within the church that is conducive to building friendships and letting them blossom.

I had a child and family worker who was very capable, and the worst thing I could have done was to micromanage her. She thrived under my leadership, and in just a year we went from one or two children in our church group to fifteen. Of course, a low-control, high-accountability approach works best when the people you're dealing with are creative, and less well when they're not. It doesn't mean those in the latter category are any less capable though – they just need a different type of leadership. I had a brilliant ordinand (a priest in training) whose output was excellent – she just needed clear instructions and wanted to be managed closely. Any project I gave her to do, she would do well, and I could always trust her to get it done, but everything needed to be discussed before she would start.

Any good leader will care for the people they lead. When I think of a good leader, I think of Jesus; he was compassionate and loving and yet also provocative and challenging, and those he led were not just his followers and disciples – they became his friends.

Chapter Ten

Family and Friends

Our family and friends are our true wealth in life. Sometimes we need to be there for them, and other times they will be there for us. You can't choose your family, but you can learn from them and what they do – both good and bad. Most likely, you'll share certain traits with them, and while unlearning the bad stuff will be hard, building on the good should be more straightforward. Friends you can choose, so be careful and wise in selecting them – and, having done so, give all you can to sustain them. Joy is only complete when it is shared with people we love and trust.

God Pod Playlist, Track 10a (Family): 'Love You Better' – The Maccabees

This song is about trying to love those closest to us better; often it's those in our family that test us more than anyone, but we will never regret showing more love to them.

God Pod Playlist, Track 10b (Friends): 'Friends (ft. Bon Iver)' – Francis and the Lights

It's probably the most obvious choice of mine, but it does feel like friendship should: warm and strong.

I was born on Christmas Day 1982 in Dublin, Ireland, along with Charles, my identical twin. Dad was a doctor, and while I was still very young, we moved to Iowa so he could complete his doctorate. I don't have too many memories about the place other than having to climb out of a window because there was so much snow stacked up against our front door. We returned to Dublin for a brief time, then moved to England to live in Northamptonshire. I guess by then I was about six.

On paper, my family are pretty intense. We've all got very different jobs: Dad is a recently retired surgeon and used to be the clinical director for the whole of Northamptonshire. My older sister is a consultant orthodontist who practises at a major hospital; my twin brother is a major in the British Army and has been to war twice; while my younger sister Victoria got a double first from Cambridge and went into law. And I'm a vicar. Not forgetting my mum who, on top of her work as a physiotherapist, did the heroic job of bringing us all up.

We're a very vocal Irish family. Nothing is off the table and *everything* is spoken about: politics, sex, religion, whatever. In my family, if someone interrupts you it means they're interested, and it took my wife – who comes from the English school of listening before speaking – a while to get used to this! In a family like mine you're always fighting for space, fighting to be heard.

While I thank God for my family, I'm also aware that we're not perfect. I'm lucky to have had parents who were around and who loved me as I was growing up, but they still got some things wrong. Now, as a parent myself, I can empathise; and I suppose most parents are just trying to better their kids and have a positive impact. But there's no manual for how to be a perfect parent – though there are plenty of books on the subject – and we often go about things blindly, making it up as we go along. I found a great freedom in my life when I realised my parents were human and carried their own scars and baggage. My dad's father had been rather distant: a product of his time, he gave little emotional support to his kids, and while they knew they were loved, it was more a cerebral statement than a *felt* experience. My mum also had some insecurity because of her up-bringing, and she carried around a feeling of not being good enough. All of us have our own self-doubts, faults and failings, and sadly we can pass them on to the people we love most and are closest to.

At its purest, family should be a safe place where love is the common currency and we are able to grow and flourish in its pres-ence; somewhere we learn to care for each other as we are taken care of, and where we can laugh and cry with those we trust completely. Loving families are like the roots of a tree – strong, deep and growing in different directions – yet no matter how far they may spread out, each family member will never forget that there is always a light burning in the window for their return. In an ideal world, families should provide meaning and belonging, unconditional love and support, and an emotional road map. We learn all our earliest lessons from our parents, and also from our siblings – even if those lessons include how *not* to behave! Good values are embedded in us from a young age, and they help us make the right choices in life; and in the event we make the wrong ones, a strong family should always be there with us, to weather whatever storm comes.

It is a wonderful thing to be part of a family, and while it takes work, I believe it's worth it. In my family, my brother, sisters and myself have a healthy competitiveness among ourselves, challenging each other to do better while also rejoicing in the successes of one another. Even though we're close, we do still occasionally have our fallings-out – siblings usually do – but we never stop loving and appreciating each other. And I'm immeasurably grateful for this.

Siblings are funny things. When my brother and sisters and I all meet up now, we banter about silly things like what my younger sister is wearing (which is always very 'loud' and expensive), or how I'm looking stronger or fatter than my brother. Sat around the table at my parents' house we talk openly about our lives, about the highs and the lows, and offer counsel to each other when we think it's needed. Sometimes our advice is welcome and sometimes it's not, but the thread that runs through all of this is that we will always be there for each other and have one another's back.

Something that has revolutionised our family dynamic is our WhatsApp group. The whole family is on it, and we use it daily to message each other funny photos, share what we've been up to, or what we've read or watched that was good. Everyone loves a good Netflix recommendation, and in general touching base with your family is a really good thing to do. It did take a little explanation for my parents to understand what instant messaging was for and how to use it, though! My mum still can't write a sentence without autocorrect changing what she actually wants to say, with the result that whatever eventually comes out makes no sense whatsoever – but as a family we have learned to translate her texts. My parents now love this new digital forum as they feel even more connected to us, as well as frequently getting to see pictures of their grandchildren. Despite the fact we are geographically scattered, we're able to enjoy a real sense of family community.

As humans, our most valued commodity is time – after all, once it's gone we can never get it back – and investing precious time into your family is really important. In my busy life spent raising two wonderful kids, caring for my flock at St Saviour's, and trying to be a good Franciscan and a loyal husband and friend, how often do I give pause to the fact that my parents won't be here forever? Many of us stick our heads in the sand about the reality that our parents will not outwit death. I recently heard an older gentleman say that if he could do anything, it would be to write a letter to his younger self telling him to spend more time getting to know his parents. We need to remember that they will not be with us forever, and cherish the moments we have with them.

That said, and this goes for many people I'm sure, families sometimes have this uncanny ability to push all our wrong buttons. I don't know whether you've noticed this when you visit your own parents' home, but I find that if I stay for too long I start to see myself regressing into old, immature ways of thinking and acting. Your childlike traits emerge, and your parents end up telling you how to live and think; and eventually the whole thing can be quite aggravating.

I've heard that the best way to survive a desert is to drink little sips of water often, rather than gulp down huge amounts at lengthy intervals. I sometimes use this principle of little and often with my family – brief amounts of time with them every few months. As an adult, and especially now as a father myself, I love going back to my parents' home. It feels refreshing and safe, but I'm mindful not to stay too long or drink too deeply. Otherwise we can start taking each other for granted and I find myself slipping back into those childish behaviours I thought I'd outgrown.

You can't force others to change their behaviour, but you can change the way you react to them. If there are destructive or childish patterns in your family that come into play when you get together, try to resist them and instead exhibit the kind of behaviour you would like other family members to copy. So when your mum says that *thing* she says that *always* gets your back up every time, or your dad does something that's consistently driven you mad, try to react differently to how you have in the past. Families know each other well, and when someone changes the way they behave it is noticed – for better or worse. If your family reunions sometimes (or often) devolve into bickering and annoyance, try instead to be the positive change you want to see in your family. They may pick up on your good intentions, and a greater shift may happen for the better.

People often say that friends are the family you get to choose. A good friend gives us an alternative view of things to balance out our own perspective. Our bonds with our fellows are deeply important to us; they define how we look at the world and how we look at ourselves. What do the building blocks of friendship look like to you? For me, they are trust, shared interests, similar values . . . A great friend reminds you of who you are, and knows you almost as well as you know yourself.

If I want to grow my relationship with anyone, I think there are three essential things that must be done (in no particular order): we should eat together, be open and trusting with each other by sharing our burdens, and laugh and have fun in each other's company!

Eating together is a necessary glue for strong bonds with our family, partner and friends. For the family it brings everybody together in one place, where they can discuss their day ahead or the day that has just passed. When I sit down with my wife and daughters for dinner at the end of the day, I think back nostalgically to when I sat at my parents' table. In my family home – that of my parents – there is a huge walnut round table, a bit like King Arthur's at Camelot. Our family gatherings are all held around that table, and it's the very heart of the house.

Eating together is so beneficial. Through the ballast of family, we build a sea wall against the tide of anxiety and solitude, and we keep it strong through the ritual of mealtimes. It's believed that families who eat together have fewer cases of depression.

When we cook for others, we can also express our love or regard for them. The care and time that goes into creating a fine meal can be a reflection of how we feel. But food is only part of eating together; it is also a time when conversation gets to flow, and when we can pause, relax and luxuriate in the appreciation of our closest ties. For children, I think it's really important they have this regular chance to feel loved and safe, as well as an opportunity for values to be passed down to them by their elders.

From a Christian perspective, Jesus doesn't give us a list of rules, but through the bread and wine of Holy Communion he grants us a meal and as we share with each other, we share in him and with him. I find it interesting that every major faith recognises the power of the meal and has teachings on when to eat, what to eat and what not to eat.

Let's think about the second key ingredient for friendship – sharing our burdens. You often hear the phrase 'A problem shared is a problem halved'. And it's so true when it pertains to a worry you're shouldering. When we trust someone else to hear our troubles, it is both a gift and an invitation. We are giving them the gift of seeing us exposed, and we are inviting them into our real world – not the perfect one we might try to display to everyone else or on Instagram. It takes trust to share something so personal about yourself with another person, and it pays off when they share something in return.

I believe this sharing of burdens marks the beginning of true friendship. Trust is perhaps the most important seam in the bedrock of fellowship. Think back to those early conversations with your closest friends, if you can. Do you remember the moment when one of you took a chance and let out something deep about yourself? The other person probably quickly followed with their own disclosure. We bond more deeply when we share our vulnerabilities and weaknesses, not our strengths and achievements, and it is to those we feel we trust that we pour them out. My closest friends are those with whom, in any given conversation, the subject of health and our emotions can be brought up as easily as talking about the weather. I find I form new friendships when I encounter honesty in others, and meet people who are not afraid to admit to and share their vulnerabilities.

Finally, for me, the third key ingredient is laughter. Someone who makes you smile can turn your mood around with their presence. When we laugh we release dopamine, and so it follows that we feel content in the company of someone who makes us smile a lot. That's not to say we should just choose friends who make us laugh. Some friends are more serious, or only let their guard down once they feel comfortable. And you may find as the years go by that certain friends you used to find amusing no longer tickle you in the way they once did. Maybe that's because you no longer have the same things in common, or maybe you have drifted apart. Perhaps one of you has moved on to another stage in your life and your priorities have changed, while the other seems to have stayed more or less in the same place. Friendships, while never transactional, are about give and take. It's important to listen to one another, and be there for each other as a trusted friend. Life can throw curveballs at us, and it is in the difficult times that we discover who our real friends are – and can more clearly see those who are only there for us in times of fair weather.

Not all friendships will last forever, and although we need to be mindful of fair-weather friends, other friendships may just be meant for a season of your life – and that's okay. Think about friends from your past, from your school or home town. At the time you probably cared for them greatly and saw them often, but perhaps life has carried them in different directions to your own.

Our relationships can have a tremendous impact on our lives, but our lives can also impact our friendships. In your teens and twenties, you'll find you have so many friends that it's sometimes hard to keep up with them all. As your thirties advance and life gets busier with work and family responsibilities, you may find you have less and less time for more peripheral friendships, and gradually your social circle is naturally whittled down to a smaller group. This is totally normal and nothing to worry about; it happens to a lot of people and, as time goes on, you may find the numbers dwindle further still, to a special few who you would do anything for and vice versa.

There's a line in Proverbs 27:10 that says 'Better is a neighbour who is near than a brother who is far away.' I've always taken this to mean that, although you may have really special people that you feel emotionally close to in your life, you also need friendships that are literally nearby and close to you. When Jenny and I became new parents, we really valued meeting other new parents in our area. As is often the way, our world contracted while we learned to care for our new baby, and it was great to make like-minded local friends who knew what we were experiencing.

Each friendship is unique, and different friendships can be formed through various points of connection. For instance, I have a friendship that is very much based on a shared sense of humour. We laugh at very similar things, but we see the world very differently to each other and make very different decisions. This friendship is not centred on 'deep chats', and instead is anchored in our shared experiences and a mutual enjoyment of one another's company. It's a very precious friendship, and although I wouldn't necessarily go to them first in emotionally heavy times, that doesn't make them any less of a friend.

Sometimes you may try to meet up with an old friend who lives far away, and perhaps it just keeps getting rearranged and pushed back over a few months. Although you love them and will keep trying to rearrange the catch-up, it's worth investing more time and energy in those friends who you can actually easily see too. I believe there's something in not weighing every friendship to see whether it will be a 'forever' friendship. There is great joy to be found in just appreciating that person and their friendship in the moment you're lucky to have it.

We're not born to be islands; humans are made for relationships. We make sense of ourselves and the world around us through our close association with others. On an emotional level, we need relationships with other people to have a healthy understanding of ourselves. But while there are good relationships – those that build us up, encourage us and help us to be the best version of ourselves – there are of course those that can tear us down, strip us of our self-worth and sap our positivity.

Imagine you're catching up with an old friend. When you say goodbye, you realise that they haven't taken the time to check how you are and, now you think about it, haven't done so in a long time. It's a sad and sinking feeling – the moment you realise you've grown apart or lost that special connection. Where once there was trust and openness, now there is just awkward small talk and one-sided interest. We may continue to entertain this kind of friendship because we've known the person for a long time – because they remind us of our past and there is so much shared history. But we have to be honest with ourselves when a person's company leaves us with a sour aftertaste or feeling diminished. Sometimes we need to compassionately let go of friendships that have run their course, though this can be a hard thing to do. If you can, gracefully withdraw from them; if you possess the strength, let them know why. Think of a bush that needs to be dead-headed: as you set about removing the dead flowers, you make space for new buds to bloom. Letting go of certain connections lets other meaningful friendships blossom and grow.

When I am faced with difficult people, I try to have a hard skin and a soft heart. What I mean is, I try not to let their words or actions negatively affect my inner disposition or enter into or harm my soul. I refuse to let anyone make me bitter, resentful or angry. Although it might be easier to close myself off and react to difficult people in kind, I try my best to keep a loving and open heart towards them, and to treat them with compassion. We all have people in our lives who affect us in different ways – for better or for worse. Take care of your heart. Try to surround yourself with people who support you and build you up, who you can be comfortably vulnerable with and whose company brings you joy. Treasure and protect them. Let them know you value their presence in your life – and that, like you, they are loved.

Chapter Eleven

Love

The most exciting adventure you will ever have is falling in love. It's as if you suddenly become aware of the reason for all things, and it is terrifying and exhilarating as you realise it will either make you or break you. Romantic love burns the brightest and at the highest temperature, but loving friendships sustain us and endure through the coldest winters. Whatever else you do in life, love and love well – for it is an eternal substance. All will pass away, but love will remain; God is love, and those who live in love live in God.

God Pod Playlist, Track 11: 'May I Have This Dance?' – Francis and the Lights

This feels like taking a risk and going all in, not knowing the end but trusting in the beginning. If not for love, what are we willing to take risks for?

Being in love is one of life's most exciting adventures. To experience the sensation of finding someone we find endlessly fascinating is an unrivalled joy, and makes our higher senses feel utterly alive and connected with the world. For millennia, poets and playwrights have rhapsodised about love as a rare and precious thing. Although finding the right person that you want to be with for the rest of your life is not as easy as the movies make it seem, once you do find that special someone it feels as if you have happened upon something miraculous and divine. Love brings out the best in us — and sometimes the worst, too, if one person loves less than the other.

Depending on where you live, meeting people is not always easy. By matching your interests to find someone who is compatible with you, online dating sites can really help. While some people use online dating to facilitate one-night stands or casual hook-ups, they can also be used to find genuine, lasting love. In fact, I have conducted a number of weddings where the bride and groom met through online dating or apps. In this increasingly online world, I believe we need not be nervous about the internet but should instead choose to use it in good ways.

Just like friendships, romantic relationships can only flourish when both of you allow yourself to be vulnerable and open with one another. Connection is made not through showing off our strengths, but sharing our weaknesses. My wife Jenny knows and loves me more than anyone else I've ever known. That is in part due to her knowing all my faults and loving me through them. When we first fell in love it was exciting but also terrifying, as I realised she could break my heart if she were to step away from my love and deny me hers.

Many of us would like to believe that one day we'll just bump into the love of our life – our soulmate – with whom we will fall mutually in love at first sight, or thereabouts. But a soulmate is discovered through the process of getting to know someone and discovering you have a great deal in common. It is not just a cosmetic case of finding a stranger irresistible because they are handsome or beautiful. Often a common occurrence in children's animated films, love at first sight is not equal to the common reality most of us experience. Delightful though these fairy-tale films are, I wonder whether the 'Disney lens' is an outdated one that is setting our children up for a fall. That fantasy of love at first sight and happily ever after is slowly changing thanks to newer stories such as *Frozen*, the plot of which critiques falling in love with someone you've only just met. But the impact of this shift will take time, and for every *Beauty and the Beast* – where Belle learns that beauty is skin-deep and real love is about getting to know someone's heart and the nobility and kindness of their character – there are fifty other kids' movies selling a false reality: namely that a square chin or pair of red-rose lips is the right criteria when choosing a partner. Love, if it is to survive beyond its initial blossoming and honeymoon period, needs constant maintenance, understanding and effort from both sides.

Thanks to social conditioning through movies, even as adults we succumb to the false notion that, having found the right person, you will always be in unconditional love and there will never be so much as a wrinkle in the future. I call this the 'Notting Hill lie', after the film in which Hugh Grant play a lowly bookshop owner who falls in love with a world-famous actress, played by Julia Roberts. Despite the polarity of their very different lives, love reigns eternal, conquers all, and they both live happily ever after. In Notting Hill, of course.

I often think of love as a garden. Imagine you and your other half have a patch of land, and you want to grow things in it like flowers, fruit and vegetables. At first you both work at it, you turn the soil over and plant things. Soon the grass grows, the flowers bloom, and for a time you can simply enjoy the garden. After a while though, you need to do some maintenance here and there, like pulling out the occasional weed, trimming the grass and regular watering. You need to invest time in it, otherwise what was once beautiful can quickly become overgrown, with the weeds choking the flowers. And the longer you leave it, the harder it is to get back to a place where you can just enjoy the garden. So many relationships and marriages break down because we don't spend the necessary time tending to our shared garden.

I think it's really important that we don't place all our happiness in life in the hands of another person. By this I don't mean that we should hold anything back in our love for our partner, but that I feel there is a danger in believing you will only be happy when you are joined to somebody else. First, you need to find contentment in your own company, as the only person who can truly help you achieve satisfaction in yourself is you. You shouldn't rely on someone else to complete you, as doing so can lead to co-dependency and a false idolisation of the other person. This happens when one person clings to the other and, like a see-saw overly weighted on one side, a lack of equilibrium occurs in the relationship. There is less give and take, and their sense of inferiority in comparison to their beloved can bring out their insecurities. A relationship should be equal, and on a completely even footing.

The stronger we build the foundations of our own self, the less we need to depend on or cling to the one we love. We shouldn't lose our own identity in a relationship, but instead respect each other's individuality. The Lebanese poet Kahlil Gibran, in his poem on marriage, suggests we should have spaces in our togetherness that allow us to be alone with our solitary selves, in order to celebrate and appreciate our choice to come together. He talks about how an oak and a cypress tree cannot properly flourish in one another's shadow, and how each requires their own patch of sun and the space to grow to their full potential. We should never feel chained to or stifled by our partner – but rather, like the oak tree and the cypress tree, feel like we can stand sufficiently apart from one another and maintain that all-important room to continue growing in ourselves.

We sacrifice selfishness on the altar of love – and with it, self-protection and caution. Matters of the heart can be unpredictable and uncontrollable and, on this dopamine rollercoaster, we feel highs so sublime we get a taste of what heaven might be like – the celestial here on earth. But the flipside is we can fall so hard that our hearts actually ache when they feel broken by love. When Alfred, Lord Tennyson wrote, ''Tis better to have loved and lost / Than never to have loved at all', he knew that to fall in love means to open yourself up to pain and heartbreak. But he also knew that love is worth the risk.

The more you give of yourself and the higher your love soars, the bigger the drop is should things fall apart. But we cannot lead our lives with stabilisers on, or hold ourselves back through fear. The magic of love is that it unfetters us, lights up our souls and brings out the best parts of our nature. Through it, we experience the joy of giving, patience and passion, and step outside of our solitary selves.

At its best, love is when you feel comfortable enough to completely let your guard down, and with it any social masks or pretensions you've constructed for the outside world. Real love allows you to be yourself without fear of rejection, and involves an understanding between two people that is so rich that they feel safe and at home with the other – as if they were, as Aristotle said, one soul in two people.

When Jenny and I go through difficult periods in our marriage, it's usually because we have forgotten to hang out and have fun together and have allowed 'life' to get in the way of 'us'. It's crazy how easy it can be to prioritise everything else over the people we love the most. We try to go on dates once a week, where possible, doing things that we both enjoy, and taking the time to catch our breath and be happy in each other's space again. Sometimes we have spontaneous dance parties in our lounge, where we turn the music up loud and dance with each other. It's our thing and I know Jenny loves it. We work at our love, because its rewards are far beyond anything else this world can offer, and we help bring out the best in each other.

Every loving relationship is a colourful journey of struggle, adventure, friendship, comfort, tragedy (occasionally), spite, warmth, suspicion, attraction, trust, and so many other inescapably human things. Nothing stays the same and nor is anything imperishable, including love. When you and your partner take time out from life's stresses and go away for a few days together, one of the most pleasant surprises is the realisation that you're still the same people who fell in love so many moons ago – you just look a little different, perhaps with a few more wrinkles and grey hairs here and there.

Research suggests that when couples first get together, before the arrival of kids, we spend at least fifteen hours per week in each other's pockets. In the beginning, we're more curious, well-behaved, hungry for detail and are better listeners. Gradually, this selfless investment can wear off and we forget to ask questions because we think we already know all the answers; we've heard the stories before, and we believe there is nothing new to learn about that person. Lazy long-term relationships can feel like ships passing in the night. And it can be a very lonely and long night if we're not careful. When we neglect to invest time in our relationship, we drift apart, and with the drift come negative feelings: mistrust, apathy and resentment. If we're not careful, we can end up like arid and cold husks. Summing up this 'domestic drift' with acidic accuracy, W. H. Auden wrote: 'The glacier knocks in the cupboard, / The desert sighs in the bed, / And the crack in the tea-cup opens, / A lane to the land of the dead.' These glaciers and deserts are inhospitable, erosive things, and it can be very difficult to find a way back from them – especially if they have been left to grow too great in size. Unless we regularly conduct health checks in our relationship, a creeping neglect can set in. In our overly complex lives, juggling myriad balls, we often forget to water what is probably the most important plant in the house.

When a relationship finishes, people often feel lost when they find themselves on their own, but, little by little, they begin to rediscover things about themselves that perhaps got lost or forgotten about in their relationship. For many of us, becoming single again can feel like coming back to and rediscovering ourselves, and it is nothing to feel ashamed of. It's much better to be on your own than stuck in a relationship you're afraid to leave or which doesn't make you happy.

Some of the best times in my life were when I was single. Being happy on your own is a necessary skill that all of us should practise. Many of us dread the thought of being on our own, only to discover that it's really not that bad after all. During this time, we get to know ourselves better, learning what makes us tick and really thinking about our desires and plans for the future. It's important to be comfortable with your own company and in your own skin – because, like it or not, you're stuck with yourself for the rest of your life. You may as well get to know and love yourself.

When I was twenty-one, I split up from a girl I'd been seeing, and I needed some time to reconnect with myself and find out who I was. I had just bought a house and I was in a stable job with a good career path ahead of me, but I was grossly unhappy! It was at this moment that I felt I really needed to get away. Being single allowed me the freedom to challenge myself and to go to Africa without having to answer to anyone, and it was there that I felt my calling to become a priest sing loudly.

When we are on our own, we can embrace life's surprising twists and adventures more readily than we can when we are in a relationship and another person needs to be considered and compromises reached. But with only yourself to fall back on, you may also find you have to push yourself a little more socially and make more of an effort. This will only help you grow in confidence. Revel in your solo time, go on as many adventures as you can, listen to your inner voice and immerse yourself in new things – whatever it may be that makes you feel good in your soul.

As a priest, I can't finish writing a chapter on love without talking about God, who the scripture says *is* love. Jesus's teaching on love is, I think, the purest teaching the world has ever recieved: 'A new command I give you: love one another. As I have loved you, so you must love one another. By this all people will know that you are my disciples, if you love one another' (John 13:34–35).

We are called to – even commanded to – love each other, and this is not some passing comment by Jesus as he walks in the fields with one of the disciples; he says it to them during the Last Supper, in his final address before he is betrayed and crucified. So, what does it look like to love as Jesus loved? Perhaps we should look to John, who of all the apostles was the closest to Jesus. In his gospel, he writes:

> This is how we know what love is: Jesus Christ laid down his life for us. And we ought to lay down our lives for our brothers and sisters. If anyone has material possessions and sees a brother or sister in need but has no pity on them, how can the love of God be in that person? Dear children, let us not love with words or speech but with actions and in truth.

John believed that we truly know what love is because, out of love, Jesus laid down his life for us. For John, in order to love as Jesus loves, we should also be willing to lay down our lives for our brothers and sisters. Though by modern measures this may seem extreme, we can understand it as that fierce love a parent has for their child, or the protective love we feel towards those closest to us: people you would take a bullet for, as the saying goes. Our world can be greedy and full of shallow self-interest, but God calls for us to care for others and to act with generosity and humility.

John links this great and powerful love with our ability to feel pity and compassion for others around us – even strangers – and says that to love others as Jesus loved us is to love through selfless and compassionate actions and not just through words. When people experience a loving, welcoming atmosphere or an interaction of care, it inspires them to love better. Love begets love and inspires it in others.

Love is not a passive act. It requires presence and intention, and we see this when John calls for us not to love with words or speech but with actions. It's very easy to claim to love someone or something, but the truth of your feelings is revealed by your daily actions. If they are consistently considerate, thoughtful, generous and loving, then your actions speak to and affirm the truth behind your words. When not backed by loving actions, loving words and speeches may come across as merely lip service to love.

When I think about Jesus, I realise that he loves despite interruption but also *because* of it. His ministry sometimes seems to be a series of interruptions from people asking for his help while he's on his way to somewhere else: Bartimaeus by the roadside; Zacchaeus up a tree; the Samaritan woman at the well. Jesus has other places to go and other people to see, and yet he always stops.

We can all love better, so let's look to love well, to be inspired to love and inspire love in others, to not love passively but to approach love with active involvement, and to love and care for others. In our day-to-day lives, as we go about our business, we should be willing to be interrupted, and welcome the diversions that allow us to make time to love those around us.

Chapter Twelve

Death and Grief

Grief is part of our inheritance as humans, a shroud which we will all have to wear for a time. It will dull the light to our eyes and mask us a little to the world around us, but we can after a while remove that shroud and be restored to the fresh air and the light. Death will visit us but we need not fear it; we should know that death is no bogeyman standing around the corner waiting to grab and put in his sack anyone he can. Death is a part of life that allows for resurrection; death is not the end of things, only a gateway into the next part of our eternal lives. So, don't be afraid – tip your hat, pay your respects and know that you are loved past death.

God Pod Playlist, Track 12a: 'When the Party's Over' – Billie Eilish

With the beautiful melancholic voice layered with haunting tones, this song conjures the feeling of lying in a desert at night looking up at the canopy of space; its beauty only matched by its starkness.

God Pod Playlist, Track 12b: 'Everything I Wanted' – Billie Eilish

This feels like death and grief in some strange way to me.

For many of us, the first death we experience is that of a grandparent. I saw my grandfather's body in his casket when I was nineteen years old. It was a turning point in my faith because, as I looked at him, there was little difference between him and a wax figure. There seemed nothing left but an empty husk, and I knew that wasn't him anymore; my grandfather had been a person of presence and light. Every part of me screamed with certainty: 'He is somewhere else. There is another place.'

I met death one afternoon in Tanzania. I'd just picked up a couple of missionaries from the airport, and we were well into the nine-hour drive back to our mission. As we came over the brow of a hill, people were running towards us wide-eyed and screaming. Then we saw violent-looking skid marks on the ground, and an overturned truck that had just collided with a bus and sent it careening down a ravine.

I told the missionaries to wait in the car, and then walked through what I can only describe as the closest thing to a war zone I've ever experienced. There were bodies and bits of bodies everywhere. As I went, I placed leaves over the faces of the dead whose eyes were still open, to give them some dignity in death. I scrambled down the hill to the bus and saw limbs enmeshed in its metal wreckage. While we managed to take some of the injured to hospital, frustratingly we could not comfort them physically because they were covered in blood and there was a high risk of HIV transmission in the region. It was traumatic. I dreamed that night, and all I could do in my dreams was cry. It was as if God was helping me process the terrible grief.

While I was in East Africa, I attended the funeral of a pastor and there were some Maasai tribesmen there. I went over to speak to them and asked how they had come to know the pastor. They said they didn't know him, but they believed that whenever you pass where death has been, you should always pause. Just like the Maasai, we should respect death but not fear it.

So how should we view death? For Christians, our heritage is that death is defeated; Jesus has conquered sin, death and the Devil. As a Franciscan, I often refer to death as 'Sister Death', thinking of it instead as a familiar someone that we all go to in the end. Death can feel sinister to many of us, as if it is voracious and has an endless hunger that is never sated. Humanity has always feared death as something that takes us against our will, or before our time. We would do better to try to let go of fear over our eventual death, and instead understand that death is an essential part of life, and something that we will all witness others go through before we, eventually, pass through it ourselves when it is our time. We need a healthier understanding of death, so that it seems less like a beast awaiting us, and more like another completely natural state that we all must pass through. As a Christian, I'm sure that death is not the end of things, only a gateway to the next part of our eternal lives. So don't be afraid, and know you are loved.

Christians believe that each of us has our 'cloud of witnesses in Heaven' – that is to say that I believe our dear and departed are in heaven, watching and cheering us on. Personally, I'm not afraid of Sister Death, but I really don't want to leave sadness behind me for my family and loved ones to deal with. Along with being born and falling in love, death is one of the most natural things that will ever happen to us. As the late, great Robin Williams famously said: 'Death is nature's way of saying, "Your table is ready."'

The shortest verse in the Bible is John 11:35: 'Jesus wept.' Although you may sometimes have heard this phrase used as a sarcastic response to another person's small misfortune, the Biblical origin of the phrase is a surprisingly positive one. Jesus wept at the death of his friend Lazarus and at the sadness of those around him, and then raised him from the dead. In this moment of great sadness, Jesus felt the sorrow and cried, and then created a miracle of joy and hope as Lazarus rose up from his deathbed, now very much alive.

I was very proud to lead the funeral service for my other grand-dad; and I made sure it was a thanksgiving to commemorate a long, well-lived life and a time that allowed us space to feel our grief as well. I wanted not only for people to feel relief that this amazing hundred-year-old person had died, and joy that he had lived so well and for so long, but also to make space to grieve the fact that he was no longer going to be around. When we weep, biological chemicals are released in our bodies; weeping works like a kind of physical purge, and afterwards we feel lightened. There is nothing venerable about keeping sadness inside us when we have a natural outlet for it through our tears. It's healthy to cry and to let sorrow run its watery course, because death is sad – but at the same time we are also capable of crying tears of happiness and joy.

On the whole, people are not as brilliant as they could be at facing death. We flee from grief and the pain that comes with it as if they are something unnatural. And yet pain is a feature of life, and a necessary component of healing. The great nineteenth-century thinker Friedrich Nietzsche believed that it was only through pain that we could come to know our real selves, writing: 'To those human beings who are of any concern to me I wish suffering, desolation, sickness, ill-treatment, indignities . . . I wish them the only thing that can prove today whether one is worth anything or not – that one endures.' Although it may seem a strange thing to wish pain on those you care most about, Nietzsche believed that anybody worth their salt had to experience a level of pain and adversity, by which they could find wisdom and peace:

Examine the lives of the best and most fruitful peoples and ask yourselves whether a tree that is supposed to grow to a proud height can dispense with bad weather and storms; whether misfortune and external resistance, some kinds of hatred, jealousy, stubbornness, mistrust, hardness, avarice and violence do not belong among the favourable conditions without which any great growth, even of virtue, is scarcely possible.

In other words, the pain we experience in life is part of what makes us human and real, and gives us layers of depth.

I'm not saying that the greater the pain, the greater the person. There are levels of pain we are not supposed to experience, and some trauma can damage permanently. However, for most of us, the pain we experience – while difficult – is the thing that leads to greater and faster growth.

My wife and I were blessed with our daughter Rose. She is a treasure and we love her. After Rose, we tried to have another child; Jenny became pregnant, and to celebrate the joyful news I took her to Florence. But when we touched down at the airport, Jenny came out of the toilets crying. She had started to miscarry and there was nothing we could do. The love and hopes we had for a future with this child were dashed. We felt an overwhelming loss. We took some time to heal and quietly hoped that Jenny would again become pregnant. And she did, but again we lost the baby.

During this time, three family members became pregnant and had their babies. We were so happy for them, but every time we saw their children we couldn't help but be reminded of our own terrible losses. Then Jenny became pregnant for a third time and had another miscarriage. The pain of all these losses was unbearable, and sometimes the things people said to us out of kindness or in an attempt to console us were not helpful. 'God has a plan for your baby, and that's why he's taken it away prematurely.' 'At least you have Rose.' 'There's a reason for everything.' It felt as if they were trying to rush us on from our sadness, taking away our right to grieve.

Karma is a fine idea: do good to others and you will have good done to you in equal amounts. But I respectfully don't roll with that. I've seen good things happen to bad people, and bad things happen to good people. I believe we live in a fallen world full of fallen things.

Recently, I received a direct message from a lady who'd suffered a heart attack and lost her unborn child. She asked, 'Why me?' – but for me there is sometimes no why, no rhyme, no reason. And maybe that's okay, as we cannot escape that we live in a broken world where things can and do go wrong. God did not mark that woman out for tragedy. Nor did he mark out Jenny and our family. We are all creative fragile beings, and with life comes random pain and suffering but also miraculous joy.

In the face of tragedy, people of faith often ask why their gods were of no help and did nothing to avert it. Speaking from a Christian perspective, if God was to intervene every time one of these misfortunes was about to happen, he'd be intervening constantly and interfering in our free will – the will to truly and freely love that is the rare gift we enjoy as humans.

I attended the funeral of a recovering drug addict who had found God and fallen in love with a woman who was herself an addict. Together, they went through recovery and got married. After he died of cancer, his wife – terrified of the spectre of death after losing her only anchor in life – killed herself. At the funeral, the priest celebrated the man's life but carefully avoided speaking of the loss and pain caused by his passing, and he did not confront the wife's suicide as the tragic event it was. I remember thinking at the time, 'If we can't get uncomfortable in church and confront the fact that this woman has killed herself, then where *can* we?' In that moment, I wanted to feel the embrace of love in the same moment as I felt the pain, but for me, by avoiding the fullness and complexity of what had happened, the service seemed weak and diluted.

We grieve better when we sense and feel truth, not when we run from it; otherwise we are pushing down trauma that will come back to haunt us further down the road. Why do we believe that we can wrap grief in a blanket of joy? It's like putting sun cream on when it's raining and cold – it's useless. But there is a way you can grieve well. Instead of running away from sadness, accept the storm as though you are Nietzsche's tree. Become drenched by the rain and know that you will get through this moment. It is tough, but there are times when we need to shiver and allow ourselves to sit with the pain; we must let it follow its course, like floodwater, purging us of sadness as it slowly drains away.

Grief can eventually restore us, but it must not be rushed. By passing through the pain and accepting the sadness, we grow in compassion and fortitude. We all need to get better at sitting with our pain and stop attempting to skip over it.

There is a great poem by Minnie Louise Haskins, entitled 'God Knows', which hangs on our wall at home. In it, one speaker asks someone for a light to shine on the unknown future, and instead of giving them one, the other person suggests they walk with faith into the darkness, where God's open hand will be waiting to guide them to safety. The first speaker trusts this advice and, taking a leap of faith, finds God waiting in the darkness for them just as the other person had promised.

In my own life when I've been through times of great pain and loss, I chose to trust God to help me get through them. I trust still that he will always be with me, and that he loves and knows me. From this place I can navigate all that the world throws my way. If you are hurting, or have lost someone, I am very sorry. You may not know how to go on. But, may I say, you are not alone – and, though it may take time, you will overcome, so keep going and don't forget that you are loved.

As a result of the Covid-19 pandemic, we are currently experiencing grief and death on a scale unseen since the Second World War. For a time, it felt as though every time we turned on the TV or checked our phone or computer, we were bombarded with news reports about new victims of the virus. Death had come to stay in our living rooms.

Many of us are still grieving the demise of our old lives from before the outbreak of the virus, when we could freely see our friends and our parents, with no mortal risk every time we went shopping. Some of us have lost family members to the virus and were not allowed to be with them in hospital when they died, nor able to give them a proper send-off. For a while, funerals were small affairs, with no more than the stipulated few family members permitted to pay their respects to the dead. I'm not sure we will ever be the same people we were before this happened. Life is different now, but the only thing we can do is try to move forward. Though for many, their future is no longer what they hoped it would be.

We sometimes bracket our understanding of grief too narrowly, as something that describes the pain one feels at the passing of a loved one, a sorely missed opportunity or the end of a relationship. But I believe that grief can also refer to the death of what could have been – our dashed hopes for the future. When a relationship ends in heartache, you grieve not just for the fine memories you made together, but also because your dreams of how life was going to be with them are now shattered. When Jenny and I lost our babies to the tragedy of miscarriage, our shared grief – though Jenny's was understandably worse than mine – was not just for the embryos that were lost, but for the loss of the future they had promised: a future where we would have brought up these babies and experienced all the joy that would have been.

We have to give each other permission to grieve well, and we must allow ourselves to fully feel what we are feeling, letting it move through us at its natural pace. Grief paints not only with sadness, but draws from a much richer palette of emotions. Sometimes as you grieve you might experience a sense of lightness or joy, a feeling you have woken up from your usual sleepwalk through life. Such moments may feel inappropriate, and you can end up feeling guilty – when actually you needn't feel bad. Instead, accept that, as you pass through the cycles of grief, you will sometimes feel things other than sadness: little moments of joy when the sun shines through storm clouds. Sometimes other people try to snap us out of grief prematurely, but there is no set time frame as to how long a person should grieve, and we're all different. Nor is there a magic formula to short-cut the process.

Imagine grief like the four seasons. When a loved one passes, the initial shock and sadness feel like an icicle through the heart. But then, even in death there is light; just as you feel nothing will ever get better or fill the void, there is a stirring of hope and – leaving skeletal winter behind – the heart gradually warms with the rebirth of spring. By the time summer arrives, we feel somewhat replenished and lighter in ourselves as we approach acceptance. The autumn of our grief brings us to an understanding of what has happened as we learn how to move forward. It's as if there is a maturing within us, a new ripeness. Fall is not called the mellow season by accident!

As you move further through life, you may find yourself back in wintery thoughts for the odd spell, but this is natural and all part of grief's cycle. Feelings of pain are followed by moments of growth.

We grieve intensely because we are able to love so intensely. Sorrow reminds us to really cherish and appreciate the moments of joy when they come. So, be kind and forgiving to yourself when those feelings of pain and sadness wash over you. Give yourself time and let them flow through you. Know that you are eternally loved.

EPILOGUE

I hope that my reflections in these chapters have been helpful to you. Whether you're a Christian or not, I firmly believe that the core messages of my faith are universally transferable to anyone's life, and that our lives should be lived with kindness and consideration to others, respecting their beliefs and their right to dignity; we should show compassion for all irrespective of their status, colour of skin or creed, and take care of ourselves in the process.

Thank you for listening to me and, whether you believe it or not, you are precious and you are loved.

Rev. Chris Lee
August 2020

What people on Instagram are saying about

Rev. Chris Lee

'Your videos brought some light
back into my life today. Thank you.'

'I'm not religious but I still **love what you say**.'

'Thank you for inspiring us
to do good and be good.'

'Your 60-second sermons and words of advice
are very **reassuring and so accepting**
and easy to listen to.'

'Thank you for your words of wisdom.'

'You're easily the coolest man of the cloth
I've ever had the privilege to watch on
YouTube and Instagram.'

'I'm not a Christian but **I love the
positivity and joy** that you spread.'

'You make me feel like the world is okay
and that I am okay.'